بِسْمِ اللّٰهِ الرَّحْمٰنِ الرَّحِيمِ

In the Name of God, the Most Gracious, the Most Merciful

A BRIEF ILLUSTRATED GUIDE TO UNDERSTANDING ISLAM

Second Edition

I. A. Ibrahim

General Editors

Dr. William (Daoud) Peachy

Michael (Abdul-Hakim) Thomas

Tony (Abu-Khaliyl) Sylvester

Idris Palmer

Jamaal Zarabozo

Ali AlTimimi

Science Editors

Professor Harold Stewart Kuofi

Professor F. A. State

Professor Mahjoub O. Taha

Professor Ahmad Allam

Professor Salman Sultan

Associate Professor H. O. Sindi

Darussalam

Houston

Copyright

For Reprinting

The Web Site of This Book

This entire book, as well as more information on Islam, is available online at:

www.islam-guide.com

2nd Edition - 5th Printing

Library of Congress Catalog Card Number: 97-67654

ISBN: 9960-34-011-2

Published by Darussalam, Publishers and Distributors, Houston, Texas, USA.

CONTENTS

TITLE   **PAGE**

Chapter 3
GENERAL INFORMATION ON ISLAM....... 45

❀ ❀ ❀

PREFACE

This book is a brief guide to understanding Islam. It consists of three chapters.

The first chapter, "**Some Evidence for the Truth of Islam**," answers some important questions which some people ask:

- Is the Qur'an truly the literal word of God, revealed by Him?
- Is Muhammad ﷺ[1] truly a prophet sent by God?
- Is Islam truly a religion from God?

In this chapter, six kinds of evidence are mentioned:

1) **The Scientific Miracles in the Holy Qur'an:** This section discusses (with illustrations) some recently discovered scientific facts mentioned in the Holy Qur'an, which was revealed fourteen centuries ago.

2) **The Great Challenge to Produce One Chapter Like the Chapters of the Holy Qur'an:** In the Qur'an, God challenged all human beings to produce a single chapter like the chapters of the Qur'an. Ever since the Qur'an was revealed, fourteen centuries ago, until this day, no one has been able to meet this challenge, even though the smallest chapter in the Qur'an (Chapter 108) is only ten words.

---

(1) These Arabic words ﷺ mean, 'May God exalt his mention and protect him from imperfection.'

3) **Biblical Prophecies on the Advent of Muhammad ﷺ, the Prophet of Islam:** In this section, some of the Biblical prophecies on the advent of the Prophet Muhammad ﷺ are discussed.

4) **The Verses in the Qur'an That Mention Future Events Which Later Came to Pass:** The Qur'an mentioned future events which later came to pass, for example, the victory of the Romans over the Persians.

5) **Miracles Performed by the Prophet Muhammad ﷺ:** Many miracles were performed by the Prophet Muhammad ﷺ. These miracles were witnessed by many people.

6) **The Simple Life of Muhammad ﷺ:** This clearly indicates that Muhammad ﷺ was not a false prophet who claimed prophethood to attain material gains, greatness, or power.

From these six kinds of evidence, we conclude that:

- The Qur'an must be the literal word of God, revealed by Him.
- Muhammad ﷺ is truly a prophet sent by God.
- Islam is truly a religion from God.

If we would like to know if a religion is true or false, we should not depend on our emotions, feelings, or traditions. Rather, we should depend on our reason and intellect. When God sent the prophets, He supported them with miracles and evidence which proved that they were truly prophets sent by God and hence that the religion they came with is true.

The second chapter, **"Some Benefits of Islam,"** mentions some of the benefits that Islam provides for the individual, such as:

1) **The Door to Eternal Paradise**
2) **Salvation from Hellfire**
3) **Real Happiness and Inner Peace**
4) **Forgiveness for All Previous Sins.**

The third chapter, **"General Information on Islam,"** provides general information on Islam, corrects some misconceptions about it, and answers some commonly asked questions, such as:

- What does Islam say about terrorism?
- What is the status of women in Islam?

Chapter 1

SOME EVIDENCE FOR THE TRUTH OF ISLAM

God has supported His last Prophet Muhammad ﷺ with many miracles and much evidence which proves that he is a true Prophet sent by God. Also, God has supported His last revealed book, the Holy Qur'an, with many miracles that prove that this Qur'an is the literal word of God, revealed by Him, and that it was not authored by any human being. This chapter discusses some of this evidence.

(1) The Scientific Miracles in the Holy Qur'an

The Qur'an is the literal word of God, which He revealed to His Prophet Muhammad ﷺ through the Angel Gabriel. It was memorized by Muhammad ﷺ, who then dictated it to his Companions. They, in turn, memorized it, wrote it down, and reviewed it with the Prophet Muhammad ﷺ. Moreover, the Prophet Muhammad ﷺ reviewed the Qur'an with the Angel Gabriel once each year and twice in the last year of his life. From the time the Qur'an was revealed, until this day, there has always been a huge number of Muslims who have

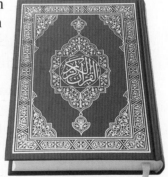

The Holy Qur'an

memorized all of the Qur'an, letter by letter. Some of them have even been able to memorize all of the Qur'an by the age of ten. Not one letter of the Qur'an has been changed over the centuries.

The Qur'an, which was revealed fourteen centuries ago, mentioned facts only recently discovered or proven by scientists. This proves without doubt that the Qur'an must be the literal word of

God, revealed by Him to the Prophet Muhammad ﷺ, and that the Qur'an was not authored by Muhammad ﷺ or by any other human being. This also proves that Muhammad ﷺ is truly a prophet sent by God. It is beyond reason that anyone fourteen hundred years ago would have known these facts discovered or proven only recently with advanced equipment and sophisticated scientific methods. Some examples follow.

A) The Qur'an on Human Embryonic Development:

In the Holy Qur'an, God speaks about the stages of man's embryonic development:

❴ We created man from an extract of clay. Then We made him as a drop in a place of settlement, firmly fixed. Then We made the drop into an *alaqah* (leech, suspended thing, and blood clot), then We made the *alaqah* into a *mudghah* (chewed substance)... ❵[1] (Qur'an, 23:12-14)

Literally, the Arabic word *alaqah* has three meanings: (1) leech, (2) suspended thing, and (3) blood clot.

In comparing a leech to an embryo in the *alaqah* stage, we find similarity between the two,[2] as we can see in figure 1. Also, the embryo at this stage obtains nourishment from the blood of the mother, similar to the leech, which feeds on the blood of others.[3]

The second meaning of the word *alaqah* is "suspended thing." This is what we can see in figures 2 and 3, the suspension of the embryo, during the *alaqah* stage, in the womb of the mother.

---

(1) Please note that what is between these special brackets ❴...❵ in this book is only a translation of the meaning of the Qur'an. It is not the Qur'an itself, which is in Arabic.
(2) *The Developing Human*, Moore and Persaud, 5th ed., p. 8.
(3) *Human Development as Described in the Qur'an and Sunnah*, Moore and others, p. 36.

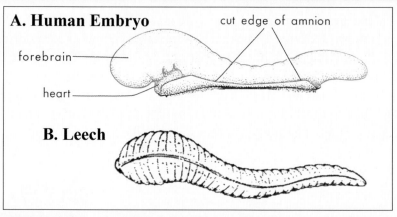

A. Human Embryo

cut edge of amnion

forebrain

heart

B. Leech

Figure 1: Drawings illustrating the similarities in appearance between a leech and a human embryo at the *alaqah* stage. (Leech drawing from *Human Development as Described in the Qur'an and Sunnah*, Moore and others, p. 37, modified from *Integrated Principles of Zoology*, Hickman and others. Embryo drawing from *The Developing Human*, Moore and Persaud, 5th ed., p. 73.)

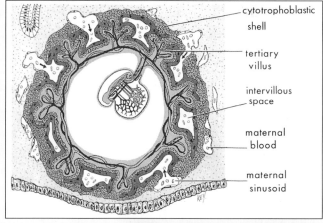

Figure 2: We can see in this diagram the suspension of an embryo during the *alaqah* stage in the womb (uterus) of the mother. (*The Developing Human*, Moore and Persaud, 5th ed., p. 66.)

cytotrophoblastic shell

tertiary villus

intervillous space

maternal blood

maternal sinusoid

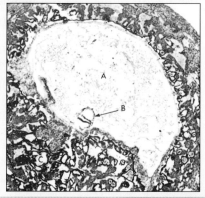

Figure 3: In this photomicrograph, we can see the suspension of an embryo (marked B) during the *alaqah* stage (about 15 days old) in the womb of the mother. The actual size of the embryo is about 0.6 mm. (*The Developing Human*, Moore, 3rd ed., p. 66, from *Histology*, Leeson and Leeson.)

The third meaning of the word *alaqah* is "blood clot." We find that the external appearance of the embryo and its sacs during the *alaqah* stage is similar to that of a blood clot. This is due to the presence of relatively large amounts of blood present in the embryo during this stage[1] (see figure 4). Also during this stage, the blood in the embryo does not circulate until the end of the third week.[2] Thus, the embryo at this stage is like a clot of blood.

Figure 4: Diagram of the primitive cardiovascular system in an embryo during the *alaqah* stage. The external appearance of the embryo and its sacs is similar to that of a blood clot, due to the presence of relatively large amounts of blood present in the embryo. (*The Developing Human*, Moore, 5th ed., p. 65.)

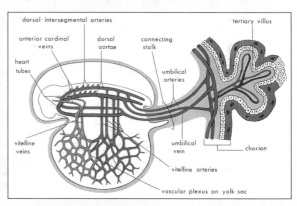

So the three meanings of the word *alaqah* correspond accurately to the descriptions of the embryo at the *alaqah* stage.

The next stage mentioned in the verse is the *mudghah* stage. The Arabic word *mudghah* means "chewed substance." If one were to take a piece of gum and chew it in his or her mouth and then compare it with an embryo at the *mudghah* stage, we would conclude that the embryo at the *mudghah* stage is similar in appearance to a chewed substance. This is because of the somites at the back of the embryo that "somewhat resemble teethmarks in a chewed substance."[3] (see figures 5 and 6).

How could Muhammad ﷺ have possibly known all this about fourteen hundred years ago, when scientists have only recently discovered this using advanced equipment and powerful microscopes which did not exist at that time? Hamm and

(1) *Human Development as Described in the Qur'an and Sunnah*, Moore and others, pp. 37-38.
(2) *The Developing Human*, Moore and Persaud, 5th ed., p. 65.
(3) *The Developing Human*, Moore and Persaud, 5th ed., p. 8.

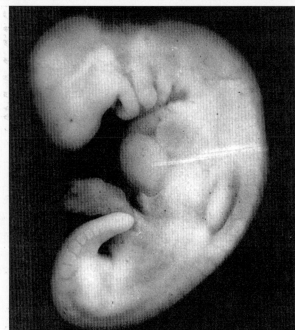

Figure 5: Photograph of a 28-day-old embryo at the *mudghah* stage. The embryo at this stage is similar in appearance to a chewed substance, because the somites at the back of the embryo somewhat resemble teeth marks in a chewed substance. The actual size of the embryo is 4 mm. (*The Developing Human*, Moore and Persaud, 5th ed., p. 82, from Professor Hideo Nishimura, Kyoto University, Kyoto, Japan.)

Chapter 1
Some Evidence for the Truth of Islam

Figure 6: When comparing the appearance of an embryo at the *mudghah* stage with a piece of gum that has been chewed, we find similarity between the two.

A) Drawing of an embryo at the *mudghah* stage. We can see here the somites at the back of the embryo that look like teeth marks. (*The Developing Human*, Moore and Persaud, 5th ed., p. 79.)

B) Photograph of a piece of gum that has been chewed.

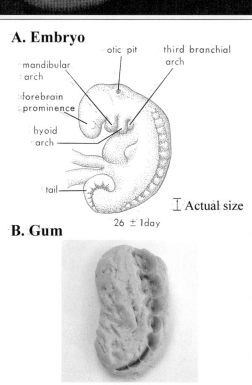

A. Embryo

otic pit
third branchial arch
mandibular arch
forebrain prominence
hyoid arch
tail

I Actual size

26 ± 1day

B. Gum

Leeuwenhoek were the first scientists to observe human sperm cells (spermatozoa) using an improved microscope in 1677 (more than 1000 years after Muhammad ﷺ). They mistakenly thought that the sperm cell contained a miniature preformed human being that grew when it was deposited in the female genital tract.[1]

Professor Emeritus Keith L. Moore is one of the world's most prominent scientists in the fields of anatomy and embryology and is the author of the book entitled *The Developing Human*, which has been translated into eight languages. This book is a scientific reference work and was chosen by a special committee in the United States as the best book authored by one person. Dr. Keith Moore is Professor Emeritus of Anatomy and Cell Biology at the University of Toronto, Toronto, Canada. There, he was Associate Dean of Basic Sciences at the Faculty of Medicine and for 8 years was the Chairman of the Department of Anatomy. In 1984, he received the most distinguished award presented in the field of anatomy in Canada, the J.C.B. Grant Award from the Canadian Association of Anatomists. He has directed many international associations, such as the Canadian and American Association of Anatomists and the Council of the Union of Biological Sciences.

In 1981, during the Seventh Medical Conference in Dammam, Saudi Arabia, Professor Moore said: "It has been a great pleasure for me to help clarify statements in the Qur'an about human development. It is clear to me that these statements must have come to Muhammad from God, because almost all of this knowledge was not discovered until many centuries later. This proves to me that Muhammad must have been a messenger of God."[2]

Consequently, Professor Moore was asked the following question: "Does this mean that you believe that the Qur'an is the word of God?" He replied: "I find no difficulty in accepting this."[3]

During one conference, Professor Moore stated: "....Because the staging of human embryos is complex, owing to the continuous process of change during development, it is proposed that a

---

(1) *The Developing Human*, Moore and Persaud, 5th ed., p. 9.
(2) The source of this comment is *This is the Truth* (videotape). Visit **www.islam-guide.com/truth** for a copy of this videotape or to view the video clips of Professor Keith Moore's comments online.
(3) *This is the Truth* (videotape).

new system of classification could be developed using the terms mentioned in the Qur'an and *Sunnah* (what Muhammad ﷺ said, did, or approved of). The proposed system is simple, comprehensive, and conforms with present embryological knowledge. The intensive studies of the Qur'an and *hadeeth* (reliably transmitted reports by the Prophet Muhammad's ﷺ companions of what he said, did, or approved of) in the last four years have revealed a system for classifying human embryos that is amazing since it was recorded in the seventh century A.D. Although Aristotle, the founder of the science of embryology, realized that chick embryos developed in stages from his studies of hen's eggs in the fourth century B.C., he did not give any details about these stages. As far as it is known from the history of embryology, little was known about the staging and classification of human embryos until the twentieth century. For this reason, the descriptions of the human embryo in the Qur'an cannot be based on scientific knowledge in the seventh century. The only reasonable conclusion is: these descriptions were revealed to Muhammad from God. He could not have known such details because he was an illiterate man with absolutely no scientific training."[1]

B) The Qur'an on Mountains:

A book entitled *Earth* is a basic reference textbook in many universities around the world. One of its two authors is Professor Emeritus Frank Press. He was the Science Advisor to former US President Jimmy Carter, and for 12 years was the President of the National Academy of Sciences, Washington, DC. His book says that mountains have underlying roots.[2] These roots are deeply embedded in the ground, thus, mountains have a shape like a peg (see figures 7, 8, and 9 on the next page).

This is how the Qur'an has described mountains. God has said in the Qur'an:

❨ **Have We not made the earth as a bed, and the mountains as pegs?** ❩ (Qur'an, 78:6-7)

---

(1) *This is the Truth* (videotape). See footnote no. 2, p. 10.
(2) *Earth*, Press and Siever, p. 435. Also see *Earth Science*, Tarbuck and Lutgens, p. 157.

Figure 7: Mountains have deep roots under the surface of the ground. (*Earth*, Press and Siever, p. 413.)

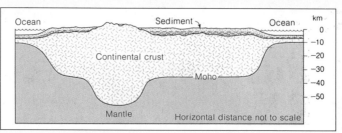

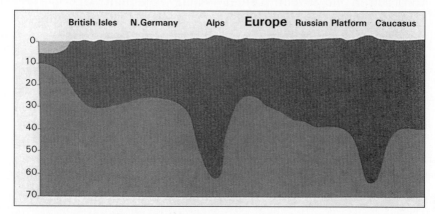

Figure 8: Schematic section. The mountains, like pegs, have deep roots embedded in the ground. (*Anatomy of the Earth*, Cailleux, p. 220.)

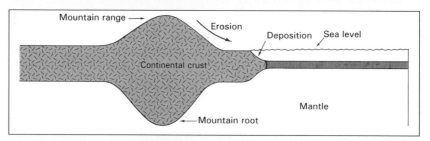

Figure 9: Another illustration shows how the mountains are peg-like in shape, due to their deep roots. (*Earth Science*, Tarbuck and Lutgens, p. 158.)

Modern earth sciences have proven that mountains have deep roots under the surface of the ground (see figure 9) and that these roots can reach several times their elevations above the surface of the ground.[1] So the most suitable word to describe mountains on the basis of this information is the word 'peg,' since most of a properly set peg is hidden under the surface of the ground.

The history of science tells us that the theory of mountains having deep roots was introduced only in 1865 by the Astronomer Royal, Sir George Airy.[2]

Mountains also play an important role in stabilizing the crust of the earth.[3] They hinder the shaking of the earth. God has said in the Qur'an:

> ❨ **And He has set firm mountains in the earth so that it would not shake with you...** ❩ **(Qur'an, 16:15)**

Likewise, the modern theory of plate tectonics holds that mountains work as stabilizers for the earth. This knowledge about the role of mountains as stabilizers for the earth has just begun to be understood in the framework of plate tectonics since the late 1960's.[4]

Could anyone during the time of the Prophet Muhammad ﷺ have known of the true shape of mountains? Could anyone imagine that the solid massive mountain which he sees before him actually extends deep into the earth and has a root, as scientists affirm? Modern geology has confirmed the truth of the Qur'anic verses.

---

(1) *The Geological Concept of Mountains in the Qur'an*, El-Naggar, p. 5.
(2) *Earth*, Press and Siever, p. 435. Also see *The Geological Concept of Mountains in the Qur'an*, p. 5.
(3) *The Geological Concept of Mountains in the Qur'an*, pp. 44-45.
(4) *The Geological Concept of Mountains in the Qur'an*, p. 5.

C) The Qur'an on the Origin of the Universe:

The science of modern cosmology, observational and theoretical, clearly indicates that, at one point in time, the whole universe was nothing but a cloud of 'smoke' (i.e. an opaque highly dense and hot gaseous composition).[1]   This is one of the undisputed principles of standard modern cosmology. Scientists now can observe new stars forming out of the remnants of that 'smoke' (see figures 10 and 11). The illuminating stars we see at night were, just as was the whole universe, in that 'smoke' material. God has said in the Qur'an:

❲ **Then He turned to the heaven when it was smoke...** ❳ **(Qur'an, 41:11)**

Because the earth and the heavens above (the sun, the moon, stars, planets, galaxies, etc.) have been formed from this same 'smoke,' we conclude that the earth and the heavens were one connected entity. Then out of this homogeneous 'smoke,' they formed and separated from each other. God has said in the Qur'an:

❲ **Have not those who disbelieved known that the heavens and the earth were one connected entity, then We separated them?...** ❳ **(Qur'an, 21:30)**

Dr. Alfred Kroner is one of the world's renowned geologists. He is Professor of Geology and the Chairman of the Department of Geology at the Institute of Geosciences, Johannes Gutenberg University, Mainz, Germany. He said: "Thinking where Muhammad came from . . . I think it is almost impossible that he could have known about things like the common origin of the universe, because scientists have only found out within the last few years, with very complicated and advanced technological methods, that this is the case."[2] Also he said: "Somebody who did not know

---

(1) *The First Three Minutes, a Modern View of the Origin of the Universe*, Weinberg, pp. 94-105.
(2) The source of this comment is *This is the Truth* (videotape). Visit **www.islam-guide.com/truth** for a copy of this videotape or to view the video clips of Professor Alfred Kroner's comments online.

Figure 10: A new star forming out of a cloud of gas and dust (nebula), which is one of the remnants of the 'smoke' that was the origin of the whole universe. (*The Space Atlas*, Heather and Henbest, p. 50.)

Chapter 1
Some Evidence for the Truth of Islam

Figure 11: The Lagoon nebula is a cloud of gas and dust, about 60 light years in diameter. It is excited by the ultraviolet radiation of the hot stars that have recently formed within its bulk. (*Horizons, Exploring the Universe*, Seeds, plate 9, from Association of Universities for Research in Astronomy, Inc.)

something about nuclear physics fourteen hundred years ago could not, I think, be in a position to find out from his own mind, for instance, that the earth and the heavens had the same origin."[1]

D) The Qur'an on the Cerebrum:

God has said in the Qur'an about one of the evil unbelievers who forbade the Prophet Muhammad ﷺ from praying at the Kaaba:

> ❨ **No! If he does not stop, We will take him by the *naseyah* (front of the head), a lying, sinful *naseyah* (front of the head)!** ❩ **(Qur'an, 96:15-16)**

Why did the Qur'an describe the front of the head as being lying and sinful? Why didn't the Qur'an say that the person was lying and sinful? What is the relationship between the front of the head and lying and sinfulness?

If we look into the skull at the front of the head, we will find the prefrontal area of the cerebrum (see figure 12). What does physiology tell us about the function of this area? A book entitled *Essentials of Anatomy & Physiology* says about this area: "The motivation and the foresight to plan and initiate movements occur in the anterior portion of the frontal lobes, the **prefrontal area**. This is a region of association cortex..."[2] Also the book says: "In relation to its involvement in motivation, the prefrontal area is also thought to be the functional center for aggression...."[3]

So, this area of the cerebrum is responsible for planning, motivating, and initiating good and sinful behavior and is responsible for the telling of lies and the speaking of truth. Thus, it is proper to describe the front of the head as lying and sinful when someone lies or commits a sin, as the Qur'an has said: **"...A lying, sinful *naseyah* (front of the head)!"**

---

(1) *This is the Truth* (videotape).
(2) *Essentials of Anatomy & Physiology*, Seeley and others, p. 211. Also see *The Human Nervous System*, Noback and others, pp. 410-411.
(3) *Essentials of Anatomy & Physiology*, Seeley and others, p. 211.

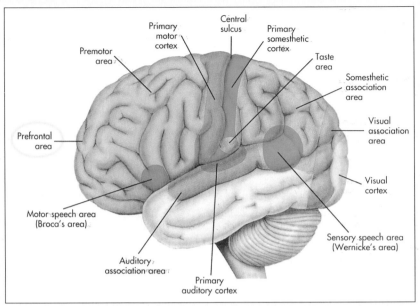

Figure 12: Functional regions of the left hemisphere of the cerebral cortex. The prefrontal area is located at the front of the cerebral cortex. (*Essentials of Anatomy & Physiology,* Seeley and others, p. 210.)

Scientists have only discovered these functions of the prefrontal area in the last sixty years, according to Professor Keith L. Moore.[1]

E) The Qur'an on Seas and Rivers:

Modern Science has discovered that in the places where two different seas meet, there is a barrier between them. This barrier divides the two seas so that each sea has its own temperature, salinity, and density.[2] For example, Mediterranean sea water is warm, saline, and less dense, compared to Atlantic ocean water. When Mediterranean sea water enters the Atlantic over the Gibraltar sill, it moves several hundred kilometers into the Atlantic at a depth of about 1000 meters with its own warm, saline, and less

(1) *Al-E'jaz al-Elmy fee al-Naseyah (The Scientific Miracles in the Front of the Head)*, Moore and others, p. 41.

(2) *Principles of Oceanography*, Davis, pp. 92-93.

dense characteristics. The Mediterranean water stabilizes at this depth[1] (see figure 13).

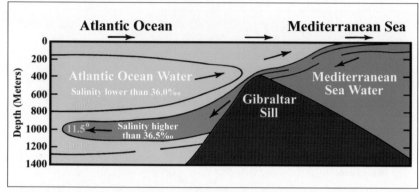

Figure 13: The Mediterranean sea water as it enters the Atlantic over the Gibraltar sill with its own warm, saline, and less dense characteristics, because of the barrier that distinguishes between them. Temperatures are in degrees Celsius (C°). (*Marine Geology*, Kuenen, p. 43, with a slight enhancement.)

Although there are large waves, strong currents, and tides in these seas, they do not mix or transgress this barrier.

The Holy Qur'an mentioned that there is a barrier between two seas that meet and that they do not transgress. God has said:

> ◀ **He has set free the two seas meeting together. There is a barrier between them. They do not transgress.** ▶ (Qur'an, 55:19-20)

But when the Qur'an speaks about the divider between fresh and salt water, it mentions the existence of "a forbidding partition" with the barrier. God has said in the Qur'an:

> ◀ **He is the one who has set free the two kinds of water, one sweet and palatable, and the other salty and bitter. And He has made between them a barrier and a forbidding partition.** ▶ (Qur'an, 25:53)

---

(1) *Principles of Oceanography*, Davis, p. 93.

One may ask, why did the Qur'an mention the partition when speaking about the divider between fresh and salt water, but did not mention it when speaking about the divider between the two seas?

Modern science has discovered that in estuaries, where fresh (sweet) and salt water meet, the situation is somewhat different from what is found in places where two seas meet. It has been discovered that what distinguishes fresh water from salt water in estuaries is a "pycnocline zone with a marked density discontinuity separating the two layers."[1] This partition (zone of separation) has a different salinity from the fresh water and from the salt water[2] (see figure 14).

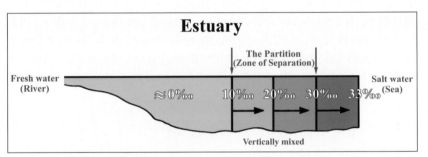

Figure 14: Longitudinal section showing salinity (parts per thousand ‰) in an estuary. We can see here the partition (zone of separation) between the fresh and the salt water. (*Introductory Oceanography*, Thurman, p. 301, with a slight enhancement.)

This information has been discovered only recently, using advanced equipment to measure temperature, salinity, density, oxygen dissolubility, etc. The human eye cannot see the difference between the two seas that meet, rather the two seas appear to us as one homogeneous sea. Likewise, the human eye cannot see the division of water in estuaries into the three kinds: fresh water, salt water, and the partition (zone of separation).

---

(1) *Oceanography*, Gross, p. 242. Also see *Introductory Oceanography*, Thurman, pp. 300-301.

(2) *Oceanography*, Gross, p. 244, and *Introductory Oceanography*, Thurman, pp. 300-301.

F) The Qur'an on Deep Seas and Internal Waves:

God has said in the Qur'an:

> ❮ Or (the unbelievers' state) is like the dark-
> ness in a deep sea. It is covered by waves,
> above which are waves, above which are
> clouds. Darknesses, one above another. If a
> man stretches out his hand, he cannot see
> it.... ❯ (Qur'an, 24:40)

This verse mentions the darkness found in deep seas and oceans, where if a man stretches out his hand, he cannot see it. The darkness in deep seas and oceans is found around a depth of 200 meters and below. At this depth, there is almost no light (see figure 15). Below a depth of 1000 meters there is no light at all.[1] Human

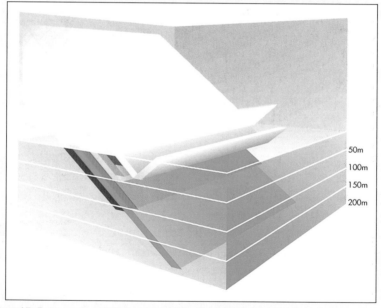

Figure 15: Between 3 and 30 percent of the sunlight is reflected at the sea surface. Then almost all of the seven colors of the light spectrum are absorbed one after another in the first 200 meters, except the blue light. (*Oceans*, Elder and Pernetta, p. 27.)

---

(1) *Oceans*, Elder and Pernetta, p. 27.

beings are not able to dive more than forty meters without the aid of submarines or special equipment. Human beings cannot survive unaided in the deep dark part of the oceans, such as at a depth of 200 meters.

Scientists have recently discovered this darkness by means of special equipment and submarines that have enabled them to dive into the depths of the oceans.

We can also understand from the following sentences in the previous verse, **"...in a deep sea. It is covered by waves, above which are waves, above which are clouds...."**, that the deep waters of seas and oceans are covered by waves, and above these waves are other waves. It is clear that the second set of waves are the surface waves that we see, because the verse mentions that above the second waves there are clouds. But what about the first waves? Scientists have recently discovered that there are internal waves which "occur on density interfaces between layers of different densities."[1] (see figure 16). The internal waves cover the

Some Evidence for the Truth of Islam Chapter 1

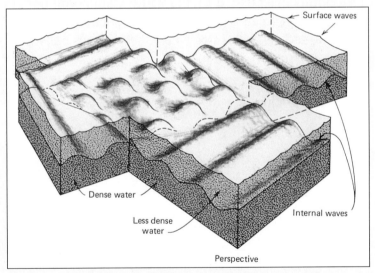

Figure 16: Internal waves at interface between two layers of water of different densities. One is dense (the lower one), the other one is less dense (the upper one). (*Oceanography*, Gross, p. 204.)

---

(1) *Oceanography*, Gross, p. 205.

deep waters of seas and oceans because the deep waters have a higher density than the waters above them. Internal waves act like surface waves. They can also break, just like surface waves. Internal waves cannot be seen by the human eye, but they can be detected by studying temperature or salinity changes at a given location.[1]

G) The Qur'an on Clouds:

Scientists have studied cloud types and have realized that rain clouds are formed and shaped according to definite systems and certain steps connected with certain types of wind and clouds.

One kind of rain cloud is the cumulonimbus cloud. Meteorologists have studied how cumulonimbus clouds are formed and how they produce rain, hail, and lightning.

They have found that cumulonimbus clouds go through the following steps to produce rain:

1) **The clouds are pushed by the wind:** Cumulonimbus clouds begin to form when wind pushes some small pieces of clouds (cumulus clouds) to an area where these clouds converge (see figures 17 and 18).

Figure 17: Satellite photo showing the clouds moving towards the convergence areas B, C, and D. The arrows indicate the directions of the wind. (*The Use of Satellite Pictures in Weather Analysis and Forecasting*, Anderson and others, p. 188.)

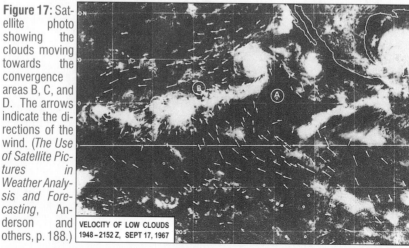

VELOCITY OF LOW CLOUDS
1948–2152 Z, SEPT 17, 1967

(1) *Oceanography*, Gross, p. 205.

Figure 18: Small pieces of clouds (cumulus clouds) moving towards a convergence zone near the horizon, where we can see a large cumulonimbus cloud. (*Clouds and Storms*, Ludlam, plate 7.4.)

2) Joining: Then the small clouds join together forming a larger cloud[1] (see figures 18 and 19).

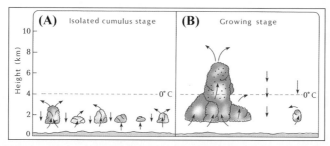

Figure 19: (A) Isolated small pieces of clouds (cumulus clouds). (B) When the small clouds join together, updrafts within the larger cloud increase, so the cloud is stacked up. Water drops are indicated by •. (*The Atmosphere*, Anthes and others, p. 269.)

(1) See *The Atmosphere*, Anthes and others, pp. 268-269, and *Elements of Meteorology*, Miller and Thompson, p. 141.

3) **Stacking:** When the small clouds join together, updrafts within the larger cloud increase. The updrafts near the center of the cloud are stronger than those near the edges.[1] These updrafts cause the cloud body to grow vertically, so the cloud is stacked up (see figures 19 (B), 20, and 21). This vertical growth causes the cloud body to stretch into cooler regions of the atmosphere, where drops of water and hail formulate and begin to grow larger and larger. When these drops of water and hail become too heavy for the updrafts to support them, they begin to fall from the cloud as rain, hail, etc.[2]

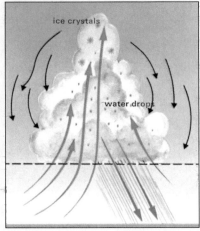

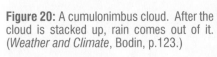

Figure 20: A cumulonimbus cloud. After the cloud is stacked up, rain comes out of it. (*Weather and Climate*, Bodin, p.123.)

God has said in the Qur'an:

❴ **Have you not seen how God makes the clouds move gently, then joins them together, then makes them into a stack, and then you see the rain come out of it....** ❵ **(Qur'an, 24:43)**

Meteorologists have only recently come to know these details of cloud formation, structure, and function by using advanced equipment like planes, satellites, computers, balloons, and other

(1) The updrafts near the center are stronger, because they are protected from the cooling effects by the outer portion of the cloud.

(2) See *The Atmosphere*, Anthes and others, p. 269, and *Elements of Meteorology*, Miller and Thompson, pp. 141-142.

Figure 21: A cumulonimbus cloud. (*A Colour Guide to Clouds*, Scorer and Wexler, p. 23.)

equipment, to study wind and its direction, to measure humidity and its variations, and to determine the levels and variations of atmospheric pressure.[1]

The preceding verse, after mentioning clouds and rain, speaks about hail and lightning:

> ❨ ....And He sends down hail from mountains (clouds) in the sky, and He strikes with it whomever He wills, and turns it from whomever He wills. The vivid flash of its lightning nearly blinds the sight. ❩ (Qur'an, 24:43)

Meteorologists have found that these cumulonimbus clouds, that shower hail, reach a height of 25,000 to 30,000 ft (4.7 to 5.7 miles),[2] like mountains, as the Qur'an said: **"...And He sends down hail from mountains (clouds) in the sky..."** (see figure 21).

---

(1) See *Ee'jaz al-Qur'an al-Kareem fee Wasf Anwa' al-Riyah, al-Sohob, al-Matar*, Makky and others, p. 55.
(2) *Elements of Meteorology*, Miller and Thompson, p. 141.

Chapter 1
Some Evidence for the Truth of Islam

This verse may raise a question. Why does the verse say **"its lightning"** in a reference to the hail? Does this mean that hail is the major factor in producing lightning? Let us see what the book entitled *Meteorology Today* says about this. It says that a cloud becomes electrified as hail falls through a region in the cloud of supercooled droplets and ice crystals. As liquid droplets collide with a hailstone, they freeze on contact and release latent heat. This keeps the surface of the hailstone warmer than that of the surrounding ice crystals. When the hailstone comes in contact with an ice crystal, an important phenomenon occurs: electrons flow from the colder object toward the warmer object. Hence, the hailstone becomes negatively charged. The same effect occurs when supercooled droplets come in contact with a hailstone and tiny splinters of positively charged ice break off. These lighter positively charged particles are then carried to the upper part of the cloud by updrafts. The hail, left with a negative charge, falls towards the bottom of the cloud, thus the lower part of the cloud becomes negatively charged. These negative charges are then discharged as lightning.[1] We conclude from this that hail is the major factor in producing lightning.

This information on lightning was discovered recently. Until 1600 AD, Aristotle's ideas on meteorology were dominant. For example, he said that the atmosphere contains two kinds of exhalation, moist and dry. He also said that thunder is the sound of the collision of the dry exhalation with the neighboring clouds, and lightning is the inflaming and burning of the dry exhalation with

(1) *Meteorology Today*, Ahrens, p. 437.

a thin and faint fire.[1] These are some of the ideas on meteorology that were dominant at the time of the Qur'an's revelation, fourteen centuries ago.

H) Scientists' Comments on the Scientific Miracles in the Holy Qur'an:

The following are some comments of scientists on the scientific miracles in the Holy Qur'an. All of these comments have been taken from the videotape entitled *This is the Truth*. In this videotape, you can see and hear the scientists while they are giving the following comments. (Please visit **www.islam-guide.com/truth** for a copy of this videotape, to view it online, or to view the video clips of these comments online.)

1)   Dr. T. V. N. Persaud is Professor of Anatomy, Professor of Pediatrics and Child Health, and Professor of Obstetrics, Gynecology, and Reproductive Sciences at the University of Manitoba, Winnipeg, Manitoba, Canada. There, he was the Chairman of the Department of Anatomy for 16 years. He is well-known in his field. He is the author or editor of 22 textbooks and has published over 181 scientific papers. In 1991, he received the most distinguished award presented in the field of anatomy in Canada, the J.C.B. Grant Award from the Canadian Association of Anatomists. When he was asked about the scientific miracles in the Qur'an which he has researched, he stated the following:

"The way it was explained to me is that Muhammad was a very ordinary man. He could not read, didn't know [how] to write. In fact, he was an illiterate. And we're talking about twelve [actually about fourteen] hundred years ago. You have someone illiterate making profound pronouncements and statements and that are amazingly accurate about scientific nature. And I personally can't see how this could be a mere chance. There are too many accuracies and, like Dr. Moore, I have no difficulty in my mind that this is a divine inspiration or revelation which led him to these statements."

---

(1) *The Works of Aristotle Translated into English: Meteorologica,* vol. 3, Ross and others, pp. 369a-369b.

Professor Persaud has included some Qur'anic verses and sayings of the Prophet Muhammad ﷺ in some of his books. He has also presented these verses and sayings of the Prophet Muhammad ﷺ at several conferences.

2)   Dr. Joe Leigh Simpson is the Chairman of the Department of Obstetrics and Gynecology, Professor of Obstetrics and Gynecology, and Professor of Molecular and Human Genetics at the Baylor College of Medicine, Houston, Texas, USA. Formerly, he was Professor of Ob-Gyn and the Chairman of the Department of Ob-Gyn at the University of Tennessee, Memphis, Tennessee, USA. He was also the President of the American Fertility Society. He has received many awards, including the Association of Professors of Obstetrics and Gynecology Public Recognition Award in 1992. Professor Simpson studied the following two sayings of the Prophet Muhammad ﷺ:

{ In every one of you, all components of your creation are collected together in your mother's womb by forty days... }[1]

{ If forty-two nights have passed over the embryo, God sends an angel to it, who shapes it and creates its hearing, vision, skin, flesh, and bones.... }[2]

He studied these two sayings of the Prophet Muhammad ﷺ extensively, noting that the first forty days constitute a clearly distinguishable stage of embryo-genesis. He was particularly impressed by the absolute precision and accuracy of those sayings of the Prophet Muhammad ﷺ. Then, during one conference, he gave the following opinion:

"So that the two *hadeeths* (the sayings of the Prophet Muhammad ﷺ) that have been noted provide us with a specific time table for the main embryological development before forty days. Again, the point has been made, I think, repeatedly by other speakers this

---

(1) Narrated in *Saheeh Muslim*, #2643, and *Saheeh Al-Bukhari*, #3208. Note: What is between these special brackets {...} in this book is a translation of what the Prophet Muhammad ﷺ said. Also note that this symbol # used in the footnotes, indicates the number of the *hadeeth*. A *hadeeth* is a reliably transmitted report by the Prophet Muhammad's ﷺ companions of what he said, did, or approved of.

(2) Narrated in *Saheeh Muslim*, #2645.

Chapter 1
Some Evidence for the Truth of Islam

morning: these *hadeeths* could not have been obtained on the basis of the scientific knowledge that was available [at] the time of their writing . . . . It follows, I think, that not only there is no conflict between genetics and religion but, in fact, religion can guide science by adding revelation to some of the traditional scientific approaches, that there exist statements in the Qur'an shown centuries later to be valid, which support knowledge in the Qur'an having been derived from God."

3) Dr. E. Marshall Johnson is Professor Emeritus of Anatomy and Developmental Biology at Thomas Jefferson University, Philadelphia, Pennsylvania, USA. There, for 22 years he was Professor of Anatomy, the Chairman of the Department of Anatomy, and the Director of the Daniel Baugh Institute. He was also the President of the Teratology Society. He has authored more than 200 publications. In 1981, during the Seventh Medical Conference in Dammam, Saudi Arabia, Professor Johnson said in the presentation of his research paper:

"Summary: The Qur'an describes not only the development of external form, but emphasizes also the internal stages, the stages inside the embryo, of its creation and development, emphasizing major events recognized by contemporary science."

Also he said: "As a scientist, I can only deal with things which I can specifically see. I can understand embryology and developmental biology. I can understand the words that are translated to me from the Qur'an. As I gave the example before, if I were to transpose myself into that era, knowing what I knew today and describing things, I could not describe the things which were described. I see no evidence for the fact to refute the concept that this individual, Muhammad, had to be developing this information from some place. So I see nothing here in conflict with the concept that divine intervention was involved in what he was able to write."[1]

4) Dr. William W. Hay is a well-known marine scientist. He is Professor of Geological Sciences at the University of Colorado, Boulder, Colorado, USA. He was formerly the Dean of the

---

(1) The Prophet Muhammad ﷺ was illiterate. He could not read nor write, but he dictated the Qur'an to his Companions and commanded some of them to write it down.

Rosenstiel School of Marine and Atmospheric Science at the University of Miami, Miami, Florida, USA. After a discussion with Professor Hay about the Qur'an's mention of recently discovered facts on seas, he said:

"I find it very interesting that this sort of information is in the ancient scriptures of the Holy Qur'an, and I have no way of knowing where they would come from, but I think it is extremely interesting that they are there and that this work is going on to discover it, the meaning of some of the passages." And when he was asked about the source of the Qur'an, he replied:

"Well, I would think it must be the divine being."

5) Dr. Gerald C. Goeringer is Course Director and Associate Professor of Medical Embryology at the Department of Cell Biology, School of Medicine, Georgetown University, Washington, DC, USA. During the Eighth Saudi Medical Conference in Riyadh, Saudi Arabia, Professor Goeringer stated the following in the presentation of his research paper:

"In a relatively few *aayahs* (Qur'anic verses) is contained a rather comprehensive description of human development from the time of commingling of the gametes through organogenesis. No such distinct and complete record of human development, such as classification, terminology, and description, existed previously. In most, if not all, instances, this description antedates by many centuries the recording of the various stages of human embryonic and fetal development recorded in the traditional scientific literature."

6) Dr. Yoshihide Kozai is Professor Emeritus at Tokyo University, Hongo, Tokyo, Japan, and was the Director of the National Astronomical Observatory, Mitaka, Tokyo, Japan. He said:

"I am very much impressed by finding true astronomical facts in [the] Qur'an, and for us the modern astronomers have been studying very small pieces of the universe. We've concentrated our efforts for understanding of [a] very small part. Because by using telescopes, we can see only very few parts [of] the sky without thinking [about the] whole universe. So, by reading [the] Qur'an and by answering to the questions, I think I can find my future way for investigation of the universe."

7) Professor Tejatat Tejasen is the Chairman of the Department of Anatomy at Chiang Mai University, Chiang Mai, Thailand. Previously, he was the Dean of the Faculty of Medicine at the same university. During the Eighth Saudi Medical Conference in Riyadh, Saudi Arabia, Professor Tejasen stood up and said:

"During the last three years, I became interested in the Qur'an . . . . From my study and what I have learned from this conference, I believe that everything that has been recorded in the Qur'an fourteen hundred years ago must be the truth, that can be proved by the scientific means. Since the Prophet Muhammad could neither read nor write, Muhammad must be a messenger who relayed this truth, which was revealed to him as an enlightenment by the one who is eligible [as the] creator. This creator must be God. Therefore, I think this is the time to say *La ilaha illa Allah*, there is no god to worship except Allah (God), *Muhammadur rasoolu Allah*, Muhammad is Messenger (Prophet) of Allah (God). Lastly, I must congratulate for the excellent and highly successful arrangement for this conference . . . . I have gained not only from the scientific point of view and religious point of view but also the great chance of meeting many well-known scientists and making many new friends among the participants. The most precious thing of all that I have gained by coming to this place is *La ilaha illa Allah, Muhammadur rasoolu Allah*, and to have become a Muslim."

After all these examples we have seen about the scientific miracles in the Holy Qur'an and all these scientists' comments on this, let us ask ourselves these questions:

- Could it be a coincidence that all this recently discovered scientific information from different fields was mentioned in the Qur'an, which was revealed fourteen centuries ago?
- Could this Qur'an have been authored by Muhammad ﷺ or by any other human being?

The only possible answer is that this Qur'an must be the literal word of God, revealed by Him.

(For more information, online articles, books, or videotapes on scientific miracles in the Holy Qur'an, please visit **www.islam-guide.com/science** or contact one of the organizations listed on pages 69-70.)

(2) The Great Challenge to Produce One Chapter Like the Chapters of the Holy Qur'an

God has said in the Qur'an:

❨ **And if you are in doubt about what We have revealed (the Qur'an) to Our worshiper (Muhammad ﷺ), then produce a chapter like it, and call your witnesses (supporters and helpers) besides God if you are truthful. And if you do not do it, and you can never do it, then fear the Fire (Hell) whose fuel is men and stones. It has been prepared for disbelievers. And give good news (O Muhammad) to those who believe and do good deeds, that for them are gardens (Paradise) in which rivers flow....** ❩ (Qur'an, 2:23-25)

Ever since the Qur'an was revealed, fourteen centuries ago, no one has been able to produce a single chapter like the chapters of the Qur'an in their beauty, eloquence, splendor, wise legislation, true information, true prophecy, and other perfect attributes. Also, note that the smallest chapter in the Qur'an (Chapter 108) is only ten words, yet no one has ever been able to meet this challenge,

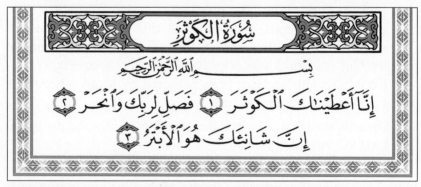

The smallest chapter in the Holy Qur'an (Chapter 108) is only ten words, yet no one has ever been able to meet the challenge to produce one chapter like the chapters of the Holy Qur'an.

then or today.[1] Some of the disbelieving Arabs who were enemies of Muhammad ﷺ tried to meet this challenge to prove that Muhammad ﷺ was not a true prophet, but they failed to do so.[2] This failure was despite the fact that the Qur'an was revealed in their own language and dialect and that the Arabs at the time of Muhammad ﷺ were a very eloquent people who used to compose beautiful and excellent poetry, still read and appreciated today.

(3) Biblical Prophecies on the Advent of Muhammad ﷺ, the Prophet of Islam

The Biblical prophecies on the advent of the Prophet Muhammad ﷺ are evidence of the truth of Islam for people who believe in the Bible.

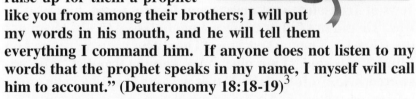

In Deuteronomy 18, Moses stated that God told him: **"I will raise up for them a prophet like you from among their brothers; I will put my words in his mouth, and he will tell them everything I command him. If anyone does not listen to my words that the prophet speaks in my name, I myself will call him to account." (Deuteronomy 18:18-19)**[3]

From these verses we conclude that the prophet in this prophecy must have the following three characteristics:

1) That he will be like Moses.
2) That he will come from the brothers of the Israelites, i.e. the Ishmaelites.
3) That God will put His words into the mouth of this prophet and that he will declare what God commands him.

Let us examine these three characteristics in more depth.

---

(1) See *Al-Borhan fee Oloom Al-Qur'an*, Al-Zarkashy, vol. 2, p. 224.
(2) See *Al-Borhan fee Oloom Al-Qur'an*, Al-Zarkashy, vol. 2, p. 226.
(3) The verses of the Bible in this book have been taken from *The NIV Study Bible, New International Version*.

1) A prophet like Moses:

There were hardly any two prophets who were so much alike as Moses and Muhammad ﷺ. Both were given a comprehensive law and code of life. Both encountered their enemies and were victorious in miraculous ways. Both were accepted as prophets and statesmen. Both migrated following conspiracies to assassinate them. Analogies between Moses and Jesus overlook not only the above similarities but other crucial ones as well. These include the natural birth, the family life, and the death of Moses and Muhammad ﷺ but not that of Jesus. Moreover, Jesus was regarded by his followers as the Son of God and not exclusively as a prophet of God, as Moses and Muhammad ﷺ were and as Muslims believe Jesus was. So, this prophecy refers to Muhammad ﷺ and not to Jesus, because Muhammad ﷺ is more like Moses than Jesus.

Also, one notices from the Gospel of John that the Jews were waiting for the fulfillment of three distinct prophecies: 1) The coming of Christ, 2) The coming of Elijah, 3) The coming of the Prophet. This is obvious from the three questions that were posed to John the Baptist: **"Now this was John's testimony, when the Jews of Jerusalem sent priests and Levites to ask him who he was. He did not fail to confess, but confessed freely, 'I am not the Christ.' They asked him, 'Then who are you? Are you Elijah?' He said, 'I am not.' 'Are you the Prophet?' He answered, 'No.'" (John 1:19-21).** If we look in a Bible with cross-references, we will find in the marginal notes where the words "the Prophet" occur in John 1:21, that these words refer to the prophecy of Deuteronomy 18:15 and 18:18.[1] We conclude from this that Jesus Christ is not the prophet mentioned in Deuteronomy 18:18.

2) From the brothers of the Israelites:

Abraham had two sons, Ishmael and Isaac (Genesis 21). Ishmael became the grandfather of the Arab nation, and Isaac became the grandfather of the Jewish nation. The prophet spoken of was not to come from among the Jews themselves, but from among their brothers, i.e. the Ishmaelites. Muhammad ﷺ, a descendant of Ishmael, is indeed this prophet.

---

(1) See the marginal notes in *The NIV Study Bible, New International Version* on verse 1:21, p. 1594.

Also, Isaiah 42:1-13 speaks of the servant of God, His "chosen one" and "messenger" who will bring down a law. **"He will not falter or be discouraged till he establishes justice on earth. In his law the islands will put their hope." (Isaiah 42:4)**. Verse 11, connects that awaited messenger with the descendants of Kedar. Who is Kedar? According to Genesis 25:13, Kedar was the second son of Ishmael, the ancestor of the Prophet Muhammad ﷺ.

3) God will put His words in the mouth of this prophet:

The words of God (the Holy Qur'an) were truly put into Muhammad's ﷺ mouth. God sent the Angel Gabriel to teach Muhammad ﷺ the exact words of God (the Holy Qur'an) and asked him to dictate them to the people as he heard them. The words are therefore not his own. They did not come from his own thoughts, but were put into his mouth by the Angel Gabriel. During the life time of Muhammad ﷺ, and under his supervision, these words were then memorized and written by his companions.

Note that God has said in the prophecy of Deuteronomy: **"If anyone does not listen to my words that the prophet speaks in my name, I myself will call him to account." (Deuteronomy, 18:19)**. This means that whoever believes in the Bible must believe in what this prophet says, and this prophet is Muhammad ﷺ.

(Please visit **www.islam-guide.com/mib** for more information on Muhammad ﷺ in the Bible.)

(4) The Verses in the Qur'an That Mention Future Events Which Later Came to Pass

An example of the events foretold in the Qur'an is the victory of the Romans over the Persians within three to nine years after the Romans were defeated by the Persians. God has said in the Qur'an:

> ❨ **The Romans have been defeated in the nearest land (to the Arabian Peninsula), and they, after their defeat, will be victorious within** *bedd'* **(three to nine) years....** ❩ **(Qur'an, 30:2-4)**

Let us see what history tells us about these wars. A book entitled *History of the Byzantine State* says that the Roman army was badly defeated at Antioch in **613**, and as a result, the Persians swiftly pushed forward on all fronts.[1] At that time, it was hard to imagine that the Romans would defeat the Persians, but the Qur'an foretold that the Romans would be victorious within three to nine years. In **622**, **nine** years after the Romans' defeat, the two forces (Romans and Persians) met on Armenian soil, and the result was the decisive victory of the Romans over the Persians, for the first time after the Romans' defeat in 613.[2] The prophecy was fulfilled just as God has said in the Qur'an.

There are also many other verses in the Qur'an and sayings of Muhammad ﷺ that mention future events which later came to pass.

(5) Miracles Performed by the Prophet Muhammad ﷺ

Many miracles were performed by the Prophet Muhammad ﷺ by God's permission. These miracles were witnessed by many people. For example:

- When the unbelievers in Makkah asked the Prophet Muhammad ﷺ to show them a miracle, he showed them the splitting of the moon.[3]

- Another miracle was the flowing of water through Muhammad's ﷺ fingers when his companions got thirsty and had no water except a little in a vessel. They came to him and told him that they had no water to make ablution nor to drink except for what was in the vessel. So, Muhammad ﷺ put his hand in the vessel, and the water started gushing out between his fingers. So, they drank and made ablution. They were one thousand five hundred companions.[4]

There were also many other miracles that were performed by him or which happened to him.

---

(1) *History of the Byzantine State*, Ostrogorsky, p. 95.
(2) *History of the Byzantine State*, Ostrogorsky, pp. 100-101, and *History of Persia*, Sykes, vol. 1, pp. 483-484. Also see *The New Encyclopaedia Britannica*, Micropaedia vol. 4, p. 1036.
(3) Narrated in *Saheeh Al-Bukhari*, #3637, and *Saheeh Muslim*, #2802.
(4) Narrated in *Saheeh Al-Bukhari*, #3576, and *Saheeh Muslim*, #1856.

(6) The Simple Life of Muhammad ﷺ

If we compare the life of Muhammad ﷺ before his mission as a prophet and his life after he began his mission as a prophet, we will conclude that it is beyond reason to think that Muhammad ﷺ was a false prophet, who claimed prophethood to attain material gains, greatness, glory, or power.

Before his mission as a prophet, Muhammad ﷺ had no financial worries. As a successful and reputed merchant, Muhammad ﷺ drew a satisfactory and comfortable income. After his mission as a prophet and because of it, he became worse off materially. To clarify this more, let us browse the following sayings on his life:

- Aa'isha, Muhammad's ﷺ wife, said: "O my nephew, we would sight three new moons in two months without lighting a fire (to cook a meal) in the Prophet's ﷺ houses." Her nephew asked: "O Aunt, what sustained you?" She said: "The two black things, dates and water, but the Prophet ﷺ had some Ansar neighbors who had milk-giving she-camels and they used to send the Prophet ﷺ some of its milk."[1]

- Sahl Ibn Sa'ad, one of Muhammad's ﷺ companions, said: "The Prophet of God ﷺ did not see bread made from fine flour from the time God sent him (as a prophet) until he died."[2]

- Aa'isha, Muhammad's ﷺ wife, said: "The mattress of the Prophet ﷺ, on which he slept, was made of leather stuffed with the fiber of the date-palm tree."[3]

- Amr Ibn Al-Hareth, one of Muhammad's ﷺ companions, said that when the Prophet ﷺ died, he left neither money nor anything else except his white riding mule, his arms, and a piece of land which he left to charity.[4]

Muhammad ﷺ lived this hard life till he died although the Muslim treasury was at his disposal, the greater part of the Arabian

Chapter 1
Some Evidence for the Truth of Islam

---

(1) Narrated in *Saheeh Muslim*, #2972, and *Saheeh Al-Bukhari*, #2567.
(2) Narrated in *Saheeh Al-Bukhari*, #5413, and *Al-Tirmizi*, #2364.
(3) Narrated in *Saheeh Muslim*, #2082, and *Saheeh Al-Bukhari*, #6456.
(4) Narrated in *Saheeh Al-Bukhari*, #2739, and *Mosnad Ahmad*, #17990.

Peninsula was Muslim before he died, and the Muslims were victorious after eighteen years of his mission.

Is it possible that Muhammad 🕮 might have claimed prophethood in order to attain status, greatness, and power? The desire to enjoy status and power is usually associated with good food, fancy clothing, monumental palaces, colorful guards, and indisputable authority. Do any of these indicators apply to Muhammad 🕮? A few glimpses of his life that may help answer this question follow.

Despite his responsibilities as a prophet, a teacher, a statesman, and a judge, Muhammad 🕮 used to milk his goat,[1] mend his clothes, repair his shoes,[2] help with the household work,[3] and visit poor people when they got sick.[4] He also helped his companions in digging a trench by moving sand with them.[5] His life was an amazing model of simplicity and humbleness.

Muhammad's 🕮 followers loved him, respected him, and trusted him to an amazing extent. Yet he continued to emphasize that deification should be directed to God and not to him personally. Anas, one of Muhammad's 🕮 companions, said that there was no person whom they loved more than Muhammad 🕮, yet when he came to them, they did not stand up for him because he hated their standing up for him,[6] as other people do with their great people.

Long before there was any prospect of success for Islam and at the outset of a long and painful era of torture, suffering, and persecution of Muhammad 🕮 and his followers, he received an interesting offer. An envoy of the pagan leaders, Otba, came to him saying: "...If you want money, we will collect enough money for you so that you will be the richest one of us. If you want leadership, we will take you as our leader and never decide on any matter without your approval. If you want a kingdom, we will

---

(1) Narrated in *Mosnad Ahmad*, #25662.
(2) Narrated in *Saheeh Al-Bukhari*, #676, and *Mosnad Ahmad*, #25517.
(3) Narrated in *Saheeh Al-Bukhari*, #676, and *Mosnad Ahmad*, #23706.
(4) Narrated in *Mowatta' Malek*, #531.
(5) Narrated in *Saheeh Al-Bukhari*, #3034, and *Saheeh Muslim*, #1803, and *Mosnad Ahmad*, #18017.
(6) Narrated in *Mosnad Ahmad*, #12117, and *Al-Tirmizi*, #2754.

crown you king over us..." Only one concession was required from Muhammad ﷺ in return for that, to give up calling people to Islam and worshipping God alone without any partner. Wouldn't this offer be tempting to one pursuing worldly benefit? Was Muhammad ﷺ hesitant when the offer was made? Did he turn it down as a bargaining strategy leaving the door open for a better offer? The following was his answer: { **In the Name of God, the Most Gracious, the Most Merciful** } And he recited to Otba the verses of the Qur'an 41:1-38.[1] The Following are some of these verses:

❲ **A revelation from (God), the Most Gracious, the Most Merciful; a Book whereof the verses are explained in detail; a Qur'an in Arabic, for people who know, giving good news and warning, yet most of them turn away, so they do not listen.** ❳ (Qur'an, 41:2-4)

On another occasion and in response to his uncle's plea to stop calling people to Islam, Muhammad's ﷺ answer was as decisive and sincere: { **I swear by the name of God, O Uncle!, that if they place the sun in my right-hand and the moon in my left-hand in return for giving up this matter (calling people to Islam), I will never desist until either God makes it triumph or I perish defending it.** }[2]

Muhammad ﷺ and his few followers did not only suffer from persecution for thirteen years but the unbelievers even tried to kill Muhammad ﷺ several times. On one occasion they attempted to kill him by dropping a large boulder, which could barely be lifted, on his head.[3] Another time they tried to kill him by poisoning his food.[4] What could justify such a life of suffering and sacrifice even after he was fully triumphant over his adversaries? What could explain the humbleness and nobility which he demonstrated in his most glorious moments when he insisted that success is due only to God's help and not to his own genius? Are these the characteristics of a power-hungry or a self-centered man?

---

(1) *Al-Serah Al-Nabaweyyah*, Ibn Hesham, vol. 1, pp. 293-294.
(2) *Al-Serah Al-Nabaweyyah*, Ibn Hesham, vol. 1, pp. 265-266.
(3) *Al-Serah Al-Nabaweyyah*, Ibn Hesham, vol. 1, pp. 298-299.
(4) Narrated in *Al-Daremey*, #68, and *Abu-Dawood*, #4510.

(7) The Phenomenal Growth of Islam

At the end of this chapter, it may be appropriate to point out an important indication of the truth of Islam. It is well known that in the USA and the whole world, Islam is the fastest-growing religion. The following are some observations on this phenomenon:

- "Islam is the fastest-growing religion in America, a guide and pillar of stability for many of our people..." (Hillary Rodham Clinton, *Los Angeles Times*).[1]

- "Moslems are the world's fastest-growing group..." (The Population Reference Bureau, *USA Today*).[2]

- "....Islam is the fastest-growing religion in the country." (Geraldine Baum; *Newsday* Religion Writer, *Newsday*).[3]

- "Islam, the fastest-growing religion in the United States..." (Ari L. Goldman, *New York Times*).[4]

This phenomenon indicates that Islam is truly a religion from God. It is unreasonable to think that so many Americans and people from different countries have converted to Islam without careful consideration and deep contemplation before concluding that Islam is true. These converts have come from different countries, classes, races, and walks of life. They include scientists, professors, philosophers, journalists, politicians, actors, and athletes.

The points mentioned in this chapter constitute only some of the evidence supporting the belief that the Qur'an is the literal word of God, that Muhammad ﷺ is truly a prophet sent by God, and that Islam is truly a religion from God.

---

(1) Larry B. Stammer, Times Religion Writer, "First Lady Breaks Ground With Muslims," *Los Angeles Times*, Home Edition, Metro Section, Part B, May 31, 1996, p. 3.

(2) Timothy Kenny, "Elsewhere in the World," *USA Today*, Final Edition, News Section, February 17, 1989, p. 4A.

(3) Geraldine Baum, "For Love of Allah," *Newsday*, Nassau and Suffolk Edition, Part II, March 7, 1989, p. 4.

(4) Ari L. Goldman, "Mainstream Islam Rapidly Embraced By Black Americans," *New York Times*, Late City Final Edition, February 21, 1989, p. 1.

Chapter 2

SOME BENEFITS OF ISLAM

Islam provides many benefits for the individual and the society. This chapter mentions some of the benefits gained through Islam for the individual.

(1) The Door to Eternal Paradise

God has said in the Qur'an:

‹ **And give good news (O Muhammad) to those who believe and do good deeds, that they will have gardens (Paradise) in which rivers flow....** › **(Qur'an, 2:25)**

God has also said:

‹ **Race one with another for forgiveness from your Lord and for Paradise, whose width is as the width of the heavens and the earth, which has been prepared for those who believe in God and His messengers....** › **(Qur'an, 57:21)**

The Prophet Muhammad ﷺ told us that the lowest in rank among the dwellers of Paradise will have ten times the like of this world,[1] and he or she will have whatever he or she desires and ten times like it.[2] Also, the Prophet Muhammad ﷺ said: { **A space in Paradise equivalent to the size of a foot would be better than the world and what is in it.** }[3] He also said: { **In Paradise there are things which no eye has seen, no ear has heard, and no human mind has thought of.** }[4] He also said: { **The most miserable man in the world of those meant for Paradise will**

---

(1) Narrated in *Saheeh Muslim*, #186, and *Saheeh Al-Bukhari*, #6571.
(2) Narrated in *Saheeh Muslim*, #188, and *Mosnad Ahmad*, #10832.
(3) Narrated in *Saheeh Al-Bukhari*, #6568, and *Mosnad Ahmad*, #13368.
(4) Narrated in *Saheeh Muslim*, #2825, and *Mosnad Ahmad*, #8609.

be dipped once in Paradise. Then he will be asked: "Son of Adam, did you ever face any misery? Did you ever experience any hardship?" So he will say: "No, by God, O Lord! I never faced any misery, and I never experienced any hardship." }[1]

If you enter Paradise, you will live a very happy life without sickness, pain, sadness, or death; God will be pleased with you; and you will live there forever. God has said in the Qur'an:

❨ But those who believe and do good deeds, We will admit them to gardens (Paradise) in which rivers flow, lasting in them forever.... ❩ (Qur'an, 4:57)

(Please visit **www.islam-guide.com/hereafter** for more information on Paradise or the life after death.)

(2) Salvation from Hellfire

God has said in the Qur'an:

❨ Those who have disbelieved and died in disbelief, the earth full of gold would not be accepted from any of them if one offered it as a ransom. They will have a painful punishment, and they will have no helpers. ❩ (Qur'an, 3:91)

So, this life is our only chance to win Paradise and to escape from Hellfire, because if someone dies in disbelief, he will not have another chance to come back to this world to believe. As God has said in the Qur'an about what is going to happen for the unbelievers on the Day of Judgment:

❨ If you could but see when they are set before the Fire (Hell) and say: "Would that we might return (to the world)! Then we would not reject the verses of our Lord, but we would be of the believers!" ❩ (Qur'an, 6:27)

But no one will have this second opportunity.

(1) Narrated in *Saheeh Muslim*, #2807, and *Mosnad Ahmad*, #12699.

The Prophet Muhammad ﷺ said: { **The happiest man in the world of those doomed to the Fire (Hell) on the Day of Judgment will be dipped in the Fire once. Then he will be asked: "Son of Adam, did you ever see any good? Did you ever experience any blessing?" So he will say: "No, by God, O Lord!"** }[1]

(3) Real Happiness and Inner Peace

Real happiness and peace can be found in submitting to the commands of the Creator and the Sustainer of this world. God has said in the Qur'an:

◀ **Truly, in remembering God do hearts find rest.** ▶ **(Qur'an, 13:28)**

On the other hand, the one who turns away from the Qur'an will have a life of hardship in this world. God has said:

◀ **But whoever turns away from the Qur'an,**[2] **he will have a hard life, and We will raise him up blind on the Day of Judgment.** ▶ **(Qur'an, 20:124)**

This may explain why some people commit suicide while they enjoy the material comfort money can buy. For example, look at Cat Stevens (now Yusuf Islam), formerly a famous pop singer who used to earn sometimes more than $150,000 a night. After he converted to Islam, he found true happiness and peace, which he had not found in material success.[3]

---

(1) Narrated in *Saheeh Muslim*, #2807, and *Mosnad Ahmad*, #12699.
(2) i.e. neither believes in the Qur'an nor acts on its orders.
(3) The present mailing address of Cat Stevens (Yusuf Islam), in case you would like to ask him about his feelings after he converted to Islam, is: 2 Digswell Street, London N7 8JX, United Kingdom.

Chapter 2
Some Benefits of Islam

To read the stories of people who have converted to Islam, please visit **www.islam-guide.com/stories** or refer to the book entitled *Why Islam is Our Only Choice*.[1] At this web page and in this book, you can read the thoughts and feelings of these people, who are from different countries and have different backgrounds and levels of education.

(4) Forgiveness for All Previous Sins

When someone converts to Islam, God forgives all of his previous sins and evil deeds. **A man called Amr came to the Prophet Muhammad ﷺ and said: "Give me your right hand so that I may give you my pledge of loyalty." The Prophet ﷺ stretched out his right hand. Amr withdrew his hand. The Prophet ﷺ said: { What has happened to you, O Amr? } He replied: "I intend to lay down a condition." The Prophet ﷺ asked: { What condition do you intend to put forward? } Amr said: "That God forgive my sins." The Prophet ﷺ said: { Didn't you know that converting to Islam erases all previous sins? }**[2]

After converting to Islam, the person will be rewarded for his or her good and bad deeds according to the following saying of the Prophet Muhammad ﷺ: **{ Your Lord, Who is blessed and exalted, is most merciful. If someone intends to do a good deed but does not do it, a good deed will be recorded for him. And if he does do it, (a reward of) ten to seven hundred or many more times (the reward of the good deed), will be recorded for him. And if someone intends to do a bad deed but does not do it, a good deed will be recorded for him. And if he does do it, a bad deed will be recorded against him or God will wipe it out. }**[3]

Chapter 2
Some Benefits of Islam

---

(1) This book is by Muhammad H. Shahid. For a copy of this book, please visit **www.islam-guide.com/stories** or contact one of the organizations listed on pages 69-70.

(2) Narrated in *Saheeh Muslim*, #121, and *Mosnad Ahmad*, #17357.

(3) Narrated in *Mosnad Ahmad*, #2515, and *Saheeh Muslim*, #131.

Chapter 3

GENERAL INFORMATION ON ISLAM

What Is Islam?

The religion of Islam is the acceptance of and obedience to the teachings of God which He revealed to His last prophet, Muhammad ﷺ.

Some Basic Islamic Beliefs

1) Belief in God:

Muslims believe in one, unique, incomparable God, Who has no son nor partner, and that none has the right to be worshipped but Him alone. He is the true God, and every other deity is false. He has the most magnificent names and sublime perfect attributes. No one shares His divinity, nor His attributes. In the Qur'an, God describes Himself:

❨ Say: "He is God, the One. God, to Whom the creatures turn for their needs. He begets not, nor was He begotten, and there is none like Him." ❩
(Qur'an, 112:1-4)

No one has the right to be invoked, supplicated, prayed to, or shown any act of worship, but God alone.

Chapter 112 of the Qur'an written in Arabic calligraphy.

God alone is the Almighty, the Creator, the Sovereign, and the Sustainer of everything in the whole universe. He manages all affairs. He stands in need of none of His creatures, and all His creatures depend on Him for all that they need. He is the All-Hearing, the All-Seeing, and the All-Knowing. In a perfect manner, His knowledge encompasses all things, the open and the secret, and the public and the private. He knows what has happened, what will happen, and how it will happen. No affair occurs in the whole world except by His will. Whatever He wills is, and whatever He does not will is not and will never be. His will is above the will of all the creatures. He has power over all things, and He is able to do everything. He is the Most Gracious, the Most Merciful, and the Most Beneficent. In one of the sayings of the Prophet Muhammad ﷺ, we are told that God is more merciful to His creatures than a mother to her child.[1]   God is far removed from injustice and tyranny. He is All-Wise in all of His actions and decrees. If someone wants something from God, he or she can ask God directly without asking anyone else to intercede with God for him or her.

God is not Jesus, and Jesus is not God.[2]   Even Jesus himself rejected this. God has said in the Qur'an:

> ❲ **Indeed, they have disbelieved who have said: "God is the Messiah (Jesus), son of Mary." The Messiah said: "Children of Israel, worship God, my Lord and your Lord. Whoever associates partners in worship with God, then God has forbidden Paradise for him, and his home is the Fire (Hell).   For the**

---

(1) Narrated in *Saheeh Muslim*, #2754, and *Saheeh Al-Bukhari*, #5999.
(2) It was reported by the Associated Press, London, on June 25, 1984, that a majority of the Anglican bishops surveyed by a television program said: "Christians are not obliged to believe that Jesus Christ was God." The poll was of 31 of England's 39 bishops. The report further stated that 19 of the 31 bishops said it was sufficient to regard Jesus as "God's supreme agent." The poll was conducted by London Weekend Television's weekly religious program, "Credo."

wrongdoers,[1] there will be no helpers." ❭
(Qur'an, 5:72)

God is not a trinity. God has said in the Qur'an:

❬ **Indeed, they disbelieve who say: "God is the third of three (in a trinity)," when there is no god but one God. If they desist not from what they say, truly, a painful punishment will befall the disbelievers among them. Would they not rather repent to God and ask His forgiveness? For God is Oft-Forgiving, Most Merciful. The Messiah (Jesus), son of Mary, was no more than a messenger...** ❭ **(Qur'an, 5:73-75)**

Islam rejects that God rested on the seventh day of the creation, that He wrestled with one of His angels, that He is an envious plotter against mankind, or that He is incarnate in any human being. Islam also rejects the attribution of any human form to God. All of these are considered blasphemous. God is the Exalted. He is far removed from every imperfection. He never becomes weary. He does not become drowsy nor does he sleep.

The Arabic word *Allah* means God (the one and only true God who created the whole universe). This word *Allah* is a name for God, which is used by Arabic speakers, both Arab Muslims and Arab Christians. This word cannot be used to designate anything other than the one true God. The Arabic word *Allah* occurs in the Qur'an about 2700 times. In Aramaic, a language related closely to Arabic and the language that Jesus habitually spoke,[2] God is also referred to as Allah.

2) Belief in the Angels:

Muslims believe in the existence of the angels and that they are honored creatures. The angels worship God alone, obey Him, and act only by His command. Among the angels is Gabriel, who brought down the Qur'an to Muhammad ﷺ.

---

(1) The wrongdoers include the polytheists.
(2) *NIV Compact Dictionary of the Bible*, Douglas, p. 42.

3) Belief in God's Revealed Books:

Muslims believe that God revealed books to His messengers as proof for mankind and as guidance for them. Among these books is the Qur'an, which God revealed to the Prophet Muhammad ﷺ. God has guaranteed the Qur'an's protection from any corruption or distortion. God has said:

> ❨ Indeed, We have sent down the Qur'an, and surely We will guard it (from corruption). ❩ (Qur'an, 15:9)

4) Belief in the Prophets and Messengers of God:

Muslims believe in the prophets and messengers of God, starting with Adam, including Noah, Abraham, Ishmael, Isaac, Jacob, Moses, and Jesus (peace be upon them). But God's final message to man, a reconfirmation of the eternal message, was revealed to the Prophet Muhammad ﷺ. Muslims believe that Muhammad ﷺ is the last prophet sent by God, as God has said:

> ❨ Muhammad is not the father of any one of your men, but he is the Messenger of God and the last of the prophets... ❩ (Qur'an, 33:40)

Muslims believe that all the prophets and messengers were created human beings who had none of the divine qualities of God.

5) Belief in the Day of Judgment:

Muslims believe in the Day of Judgment (the Day of Resurrection) when all people will be resurrected for God's judgment according to their beliefs and deeds.

6) Belief in *Al-Qadar*:

Muslims believe in *Al-Qadar*, which is Divine Predestination, but this belief in Divine Predestination does not mean that human beings do not have freewill. Rather, Muslims believe that God has given human beings freewill. This means that they can choose right or wrong and that they are responsible for their choices.

The belief in Divine Predestination includes belief in four things: 1) God knows everything. He knows what has happened and what will happen. 2) God has recorded all that has happened and all that will happen. 3) Whatever God wills to happen happens, and whatever He wills not to happen does not happen. 4) God is the Creator of everything.

(Please visit **www.islam-guide.com/beliefs** for more information on basic Islamic beliefs.)

Is There Any Sacred Source Other than the Qur'an?

Yes. The *sunnah* (what the Prophet Muhammad ﷺ said, did, or approved of) is the second source in Islam. The *sunnah* is comprised of *hadeeths*, which are reliably transmitted reports by the Prophet Muhammad's ﷺ companions of what he said, did, or approved of. Belief in the *sunnah* is a basic Islamic belief.

Examples of the Prophet Muhammad's ﷺ Sayings

- { The believers, in their love, mercy, and kindness to one another are like a body: if any part of it is ill, the whole body shares its sleeplessness and fever. }[1]
- { The most perfect of the believers in faith are the best of them in morals. And the best among them are those who are best to their wives. }[2]
- { None of you believes (completely) until he loves for his brother what he loves for himself. }[3]
- { The merciful are shown mercy by the All-Merciful. Show mercy to those on earth, and God will show mercy to you. }[4]
- { Smiling at your brother is charity... }[5]
- { A good word is charity. }[6]

---

(1) Narrated in *Saheeh Muslim*, #2586, and *Saheeh Al-Bukhari*, #6011.
(2) Narrated in *Mosnad Ahmad*, #7354, and *Al-Tirmizi*, #1162.
(3) Narrated in *Saheeh Al-Bukhari*, #13, and *Saheeh Muslim*, #45.
(4) Narrated in *Al-Tirmizi*, #1924, and *Abu-Dawood*, #4941.
(5) Narrated in *Al-Tirmizi*, #1956.
(6) Narrated in *Saheeh Muslim*, #1009, and *Saheeh Al-Bukhari*, #2989.

- { Whoever believes in God and the Last Day (the Day of Judgment) should do good to his neighbor. }[1]
- { God does not judge you according to your appearance and your wealth, but He looks at your hearts and looks into your deeds. }[2]
- { Pay the worker his wage before his sweat dries. }[3]
- { A man walking along a path felt very thirsty. Reaching a well, he descended into it, drank his fill, and came up. Then he saw a dog with its tongue hanging out, trying to lick up mud to quench its thirst. The man said: "This dog is feeling the same thirst that I felt." So he went down into the well again, filled his shoe with water, and gave the dog a drink. So, God thanked him and forgave his sins. } The Prophet ﷺ was asked: "Messenger of God, are we rewarded for kindness towards animals?" He said: { There is a reward for kindness to every living animal or human. }[4]

What Does Islam Say about the Day of Judgment?

Like Christians, Muslims believe that the present life is only a trial preparation for the next realm of existence. This life is a test for each individual for the life after death. A day will come when the whole universe will be destroyed and the dead will be resurrected for judgment by God. This day will be the beginning of a life that will never end. This day is the Day of Judgment. On that day, all people will be rewarded by God according to their beliefs and deeds. Those who die while believing that **"There is no true god but God, and Muhammad is the Messenger (Prophet) of God"** and are Muslim will be rewarded on that day and will be admitted to Paradise forever, as God has said:

(1) Narrated in *Saheeh Muslim*, #48, and *Saheeh Al-Bukhari*, #6019.
(2) Narrated in *Saheeh Muslim*, #2564.
(3) Narrated in *Ibn Majah*, #2443.
(4) Narrated in *Saheeh Muslim*, #2244, and *Saheeh Al-Bukhari*, #2466.

❨ **And those who believe and do good deeds, they are dwellers of Paradise, they dwell therein forever.** ❩ **(Qur'an, 2:82)**

But those who die while not believing that **"There is no true god but God, and Muhammad is the Messenger (Prophet) of God"** or are not Muslim will lose Paradise forever and will be sent to Hellfire, as God has said:

❨ **And whoever seeks a religion other than Islam, it will not be accepted from him and he will be one of the losers in the Hereafter.** ❩ **(Qur'an, 3:85)**

And as He has said:

❨ **Those who have disbelieved and died in disbelief, the earth full of gold would not be accepted from any of them if it were offered as a ransom. They will have a painful punishment, and they will have no helpers.** ❩ **(Qur'an, 3:91)**

One may ask, 'I think Islam is a good religion, but if I were to convert to Islam, my family, friends, and other people would persecute me and make fun of me. So if I don't convert to Islam, will I enter Paradise and be saved from Hellfire?' The answer is what God has said in the preceding verse: **"And whoever seeks a religion other than Islam, it will not be accepted from him and he will be one of the losers in the Hereafter."**

After having sent the Prophet Muhammad ﷺ to call people to Islam, God does not accept adherence to any religion other than Islam. God is our Creator and Sustainer. He created for us whatever is in the earth. All the blessings and good things we have are from Him. So after all this, when someone rejects belief in God, His Prophet Muhammad ﷺ, or His religion of Islam, it is just that he or she be punished in the Hereafter. Actually, the main purpose of our creation is to worship God alone and to obey Him, as God has said in the Holy Qur'an **(51:56)**.

This life we live today is a very short life. The unbelievers on the Day of Judgment will think that the life they lived on earth was only a day or part of a day, as God has said:

❲ He (God) will say: "How many years did you stay on the earth?" They will say: "We stayed a day or part of a day...." ❳ (Qur'an, 23:112-113)

And He has said:

❲ Did you then think that We had created you in jest (without any purpose), and that you would not be returned to Us (in the Hereafter)? So, God is exalted, the True King. None has the right to be worshipped but Him... ❳ (Qur'an, 23:115-116)

The life in the Hereafter is a real life. It is not only spiritual, but physical as well. We will live there with our souls and bodies. In comparing this world with the Hereafter, Muhammad ﷺ said: { The value of this world compared to that of the Hereafter is like what your finger brings from the sea when you put it in and then take it out. }[1] That is, the value of this world compared to that of the Hereafter is like a few drops of water compared to the sea.

How Does Someone Become a Muslim?

Simply by saying with conviction, *"La ilaha illa Allah, Muhammadur rasoolu Allah,"* one converts to Islam and becomes a Muslim. This saying means **"There is no true god (deity) but God (Allah),[2] and Muhammad is the Messenger (Prophet) of God."** The first part, "There is no true god but God," means

(1) Narrated in *Saheeh Muslim*, #2858, and *Mosnad Ahmad*, #17560.
(2) As was mentioned on page 47, the Arabic word *Allah* means God (the one and only true God who created the whole universe). This word *Allah* is a name for God, which is used by Arabic speakers, both Arab Muslims and Arab Christians. For more details on the word *Allah*, see the next to last paragraph of page 47.

that none has the right to be worshipped but God alone, and that God has neither partner nor son. To be a Muslim, one should also:

- Believe that the Holy Qur'an is the literal word of God, revealed by Him.
- Believe that the Day of Judgment (the Day of Resurrection) is true and will come, as God promised in the Qur'an.
- Accept Islam as his or her religion.
- Not worship anything nor anyone except God.

The Prophet Muhammad ﷺ said: **{ God is more joyful at the repentance of someone when he turns to Him in repentance than one of you would be if he were riding his camel in the wilderness, and it runs away from him, carrying his food and drink, so that he loses all hope of getting it back. He comes to a tree and lies down in its shade (awaiting death), for he has lost all hope of finding his camel. Then, while he is in that state (of desperation), suddenly it is there before him! So he seizes its halter and cries out from the depth of his joy: "O God, You are my servant and I am Your Lord!" His mistake comes from the intensity of his joy. }**[1]

The saying, "There is no true god but God, and Muhammad is the Messenger (Prophet) of God," inscribed over an entrance.

---

(1) Narrated in *Saheeh Muslim*, #2747, and *Saheeh Al-Bukhari*, #6309.

Chapter 3
General Information on Islam

What Is the Qur'an About?

The Qur'an, the last revealed word of God, is the primary source of every Muslim's faith and practice. It deals with all the subjects which concern human beings: wisdom, doctrine, worship, transactions, law, etc., but its basic theme is the relationship between God and His creatures. At the same time, it provides guidelines and detailed teachings for a just society, proper human conduct, and an equitable economic system.

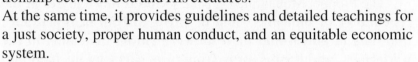

Note that the Qur'an was revealed to Muhammad ﷺ in Arabic only. So, any Qur'anic translation, either in English or any other language, is neither a Qur'an, nor a version of the Qur'an, but rather it is only a translation of the meaning of the Qur'an. The Qur'an exists only in the Arabic in which it was revealed.

Who Is the Prophet Muhammad ﷺ?

Muhammad ﷺ was born in Makkah in the year 570. Since his father died before his birth and his mother died shortly thereafter, he was raised by his uncle who was from the respected tribe of Quraysh. He was raised illiterate, unable to read or write, and remained so till his death. His people, before his mission as a prophet, were ignorant of science and most of them were illiterate. As he grew up, he became known to be truthful, honest, trustworthy, generous, and sincere. He was so trustworthy that they called him the Trustworthy.[1] Muhammad ﷺ was very religious, and he had long detested the decadence and idolatry of his society.

At the age of forty, Muhammad ﷺ received his first revelation from God through the Angel Gabriel. The revelations continued for twenty-three years, and they are collectively known as the Qur'an.

---

(1) Narrated in *Mosnad Ahmad*, #15078.

The Prophet Muhammad's ﷺ Mosque in Madinah.

As soon as he began to recite the Qur'an and to preach the truth which God had revealed to him, he and his small group of followers suffered persecution from unbelievers. The persecution grew so fierce that in the year 622 God gave them the command to emigrate. This emigration from Makkah to the city of Madinah, some 260 miles to the north, marks the beginning of the Muslim calendar.

After several years, Muhammad ﷺ and his followers were able to return to Makkah, where they forgave their enemies. Before Muhammad ﷺ died, at the age of sixty-three, the greater part of the Arabian Peninsula had become Muslim, and within a century of his death, Islam had spread to Spain in the West and as far East as China. Among the reasons for the rapid and peaceful spread of Islam was the truth and clarity of its doctrine. Islam calls for faith in only one God, Who is the only one worthy of worship.

The Prophet Muhammad ﷺ was a perfect example of an honest, just, merciful, compassionate, truthful, and brave human being. Though he was a man, he was far removed from all evil characteristics and strove solely for the sake of God and His reward in the Hereafter. Moreover, in all his actions and dealings, he was ever mindful and fearful of God.

(Please visit **www.islam-guide.com/muhammad** for more information on the Prophet Muhammad ﷺ.)

Chapter 3
General Information on Islam

How Did the Spread of Islam Affect the Development of Science?

Islam instructs man to use his powers of intelligence and observation. Within a few years of the spread of Islam, great civilizations and universities were flourishing. The synthesis of Eastern and Western ideas, and of new thought with old, brought about great advances in medicine, mathematics, physics, astronomy, geography, architecture, art, literature, and history. Many crucial systems, such as algebra, the Arabic numerals, and the concept of zero (vital to the advancement of

The astrolabe: One of the most important scientific instruments developed by Muslims which was also used widely in the West until modern times.

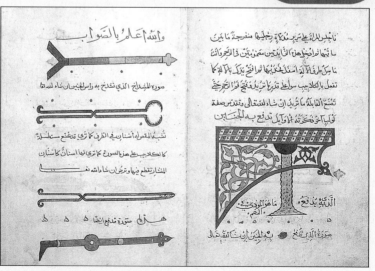

Muslim physicians paid much attention to surgery and developed many surgical instruments as seen in this old manuscript.

mathematics), were transmitted to medieval Europe from the Muslim world. Sophisticated instruments which were to make possible the European voyages of discovery, such as the astrolabe, the quadrant, and good navigational maps, were also developed by Muslims.

What Do Muslims Believe about Jesus?

Muslims respect and revere Jesus (peace be upon him). They consider him one of the greatest of God's messengers to mankind. The Qur'an confirms his virgin birth, and a chapter of the Qur'an is entitled '*Maryam*' (Mary). The Qur'an describes the birth of Jesus as follows:

> ❨ **(Remember) when the angels said: "O Mary, God gives you good news of a word from Him (God), whose name is the Messiah Jesus, son of Mary, revered in this world and the Hereafter, and one of those brought near (to God). He will speak to the people from his cradle and as a man, and he is of the righteous." She said: "My Lord, how can I have a child when no mortal has touched me?" He said: "So (it will be). God creates what He wills. If He decrees a thing, He says to it only, 'Be!' and it is." ❩ (Qur'an, 3:45-47)**

Jesus was born miraculously by the command of God, the same command that had brought Adam into being with neither a father nor a mother. God has said:

> ❨ **The case of Jesus with God is like the case of Adam. He created him from dust, and then He said to him, "Be!" and he came into being. ❩ (Qur'an, 3:59)**

During his prophetic mission, Jesus performed many miracles. God tells us that Jesus said:

❴ "I have come to you with a sign from your Lord. I make for you the shape of a bird out of clay, I breathe into it, and it becomes a bird by God's permission. I heal the blind from birth and the leper. And I bring the dead to life by God's permission. And I tell you what you eat and what you store in your houses...." ❵ (Qur'an, 3:49)

Muslims believe that Jesus was not crucified. It was the plan of Jesus' enemies to crucify him, but God saved him and raised him up to Him. And the likeness of Jesus was put over another man. Jesus' enemies took this man and crucified him, thinking that he was Jesus. God has said:

❴ ...They said: "We killed the Messiah Jesus, son of Mary, the messenger of God." They did not kill him, nor did they crucify him, but the likeness of him was put on another man (and they killed that man)... ❵ (Qur'an, 4:157)

Neither Muhammad ﷺ nor Jesus came to change the basic doctrine of the belief in one God, brought by earlier prophets, but

The Aqsa Mosque in Jerusalem.

rather to confirm and renew it.[1]

(Please visit **www.islam-guide.com/jesus** for more information on Jesus in Islam.)

What Does Islam Say about Terrorism?

Islam, a religion of mercy, does not permit terrorism. In the Qur'an, God has said:

> ❨ **God does not forbid you from showing kindness and dealing justly with those who have not fought you about religion and have not driven you out of your homes. God loves just dealers.** ❩ **(Qur'an, 60:8)**

The Prophet Muhammad ﷺ used to prohibit soldiers from killing women and children,[2] and he would advise them: { **...Do not betray, do not be excessive, do not kill a newborn child.** }[3]

---

(1) Muslims also believe that God revealed a holy book to Jesus called the *Injeel*, some parts of which may be still available in the teachings of God to Jesus in the New Testament. But this does not mean that Muslims believe in the Bible we have today because it is not the original scriptures that were revealed by God. They underwent alterations, additions, and omissions. This was also said by the Committee charged with revising *The Holy Bible (Revised Standard Version)*. This Committee consisted of thirty-two scholars who served as members of the Committee. They secured the review and counsel of an Advisory Board of fifty representatives of the co-operating denominations. The Committee said in the Preface to *The Holy Bible (Revised Standard Version)*, p. iv: "Sometimes it is evident that the text has suffered in transmission, but none of the versions provides a satisfactory restoration. Here we can only follow the best judgment of competent scholars as to the most probable reconstruction of the original text." The Committee also said in the Preface, p. vii: "Notes are added which indicate significant variations, additions, or omissions in the ancient authorities (Mt 9.34; Mk 3.16; 7.4; Lk 24.32, 51, etc.)." For more information on the altering of the Bible, please visit **www.islam-guide.com/bible**

(2) Narrated in *Saheeh Muslim*, #1744, and *Saheeh Al-Bukhari*, #3015.

(3) Narrated in *Saheeh Muslim*, #1731, and *Al-Tirmizi*, #1408.

And he also said: { **Whoever has killed a person having a treaty with the Muslims shall not smell the fragrance of Paradise, though its fragrance is found for a span of forty years.** }[1]

Also, the Prophet Muhammad ﷺ has forbidden punishment with fire.[2]

He once listed murder as the second of the major sins,[3] and he even warned that on the Day of Judgment, { **The first cases to be adjudicated between people on the Day of Judgment will be those of bloodshed.**[4] }[5]

Muslims are even encouraged to be kind to animals and are forbidden to hurt them. Once the Prophet Muhammad ﷺ said: { **A woman was punished because she imprisoned a cat until it died. On account of this, she was doomed to Hell. While she imprisoned it, she did not give the cat food or drink, nor did she free it to eat the insects of the earth.** }[6]

He also said that a man gave a very thirsty dog a drink, so God forgave his sins for this action. The Prophet ﷺ was asked: "Messenger of God, are we rewarded for kindness towards animals?" He said: { **There is a reward for kindness to every living animal or human.** }[7]

Additionally, while taking the life of an animal for food, Muslims are commanded to do so in a manner that causes the least amount of fright and suffering possible. The Prophet Muhammad ﷺ said: { **When you slaughter an animal, do so in the best way. One should sharpen his knife to reduce the suffering of the animal.** }[8]

---

(1) Narrated in *Saheeh Al-Bukhari*, #3166, and *Ibn Majah*, #2686.
(2) Narrated in *Abu-Dawood*, #2675.
(3) Narrated in *Saheeh Al-Bukhari*, #6871, and *Saheeh Muslim*, #88.
(4) This means killing and injuring.
(5) Narrated in *Saheeh Muslim*, #1678, and *Saheeh Al-Bukhari*, #6533.
(6) Narrated in *Saheeh Muslim*, #2422, and *Saheeh Al-Bukhari*, #2365.
(7) This saying of Muhammad ﷺ has been mentioned in more detail on page 50. Narrated in *Saheeh Muslim*, #2244, and *Saheeh Al-Bukhari*, #2466.
(8) Narrated in *Saheeh Muslim*, #1955, and *Al-Tirmizi*, #1409.

In light of these and other Islamic texts, the act of inciting terror in the hearts of defenseless civilians, the wholesale destruction of buildings and properties, the bombing and maiming of innocent men, women, and children are all forbidden and detestable acts according to Islam and the Muslims. Muslims follow a religion of peace, mercy, and forgiveness, and the vast majority have nothing to do with the violent events some have associated with Muslims. If an individual Muslim were to commit an act of terrorism, this person would be guilty of violating the laws of Islam.

Human Rights and Justice in Islam

Islam provides many human rights for the individual. The following are some of these human rights that Islam protects.

The life and property of all citizens in an Islamic state are considered sacred, whether a person is Muslim or not. Islam also protects honor. So, in Islam, insulting others or making fun of them is not allowed. The Prophet Muhammad ﷺ said: **{ Truly your blood, your property, and your honor are inviolable. }**[1]

Racism is not allowed in Islam, for the Qur'an speaks of human equality in the following terms:

❴ O mankind, We have created you from a male and a female and have made you into nations and tribes for you to know one another. Truly, the noblest of you with God is the most pious.[2] Truly, God is All-Knowing, All-Aware. ❵ (Qur'an, 49:13)

Islam rejects certain individuals or nations being favored because of their wealth, power, or race. God created human beings as equals who are to be distinguished from each other only on the basis of their faith and piety. The Prophet Muhammad ﷺ

---

(1) Narrated in *Saheeh Al-Bukhari*, #1739, and *Mosnad Ahmad*, #2037.
(2) A pious person is a believer who abstains from all kinds of sins, performs all good deeds that God commands us to do, and fears and loves God.

said: { **O people! Your God is one and your forefather (Adam) is one. An Arab is not better than a non-Arab and a non-Arab is not better than an Arab, and a red (i.e. white tinged with red) person is not better than a black person and a black person is not better than a red person,**[1] **except in piety. }**[2]

One of the major problems facing mankind today is racism. The developed world can send a man to the moon but cannot stop man from hating and fighting his fellow man. Ever since the days of the Prophet Muhammad ﷺ, Islam has provided a vivid example of how racism can be ended. The annual pilgrimage (*Hajj*) to Makkah shows the real Islamic brotherhood of all races and nations, when about two million Muslims from all over the world come to Makkah to perform the pilgrimage.

Islam is a religion of justice. God has said:

> ❨ **Truly God commands you to give back trusts to those to whom they are due, and when you judge between people, to judge with justice....** ❩ **(Qur'an, 4:58)**

And He has said:

> ❨ **...And act justly. Truly, God loves those who are just.** ❩ **(Qur'an, 49:9)**

---

(1) The colors mentioned in this Prophetic saying are examples. The meaning is that in Islam no one is better than another because of his color, whether it is white, black, red, or any other color.

(2) Narrated in *Mosnad Ahmad*, #22978.

We should even be just with those who we hate, as God has said:

⟨ **...And let not the hatred of others make you avoid justice. Be just: that is nearer to piety....** ⟩ (Qur'an, 5:8)

The Prophet Muhammad ﷺ said: { **People, beware of injustice,**[1] **for injustice shall be darkness on the Day of Judgment.** }[2]

And those who have not gotten their rights (i.e. what they have a just claim to) in this life will receive them on the Day of Judgment, as the Prophet ﷺ said: { **On the Day of Judgment, rights will be given to those to whom they are due (and wrongs will be redressed)...** }[3]

What Is the Status of Women in Islam?

Islam sees a woman, whether single or married, as an individual in her own right, with the right to own and dispose of her property and earnings without any guardianship over her (whether that be her father, husband, or anyone else). She has the right to buy and sell, give gifts and charity, and may spend her money as she pleases. A marriage dowry is given by the groom to the bride for her own personal use, and she keeps her own family name rather than taking her husband's.

Islam encourages the husband to treat his wife well, as the Prophet Muhammad ﷺ said: { **The best among you are those who are best to their wives.** }[4]

---

(1) i.e. oppressing others, acting unjustly, or doing wrong to others.
(2) Narrated in *Mosnad Ahmad*, #5798, and *Saheeh Al-Bukhari*, #2447.
(3) Narrated in *Saheeh Muslim*, #2582, and *Mosnad Ahmad*, #7163.
(4) Narrated in *Ibn Majah*, #1978, and *Al-Tirmizi*, #3895.

Mothers in Islam are highly honored. Islam recommends treating them in the best way. **A man came to the Prophet Muhammad ﷺ and said: "O Messenger of God! Who among the people is the most worthy of my good companionship?" The Prophet ﷺ said: { Your mother. } The man said: "Then who?" The Prophet ﷺ said: { Then your mother. } The man further asked: "Then who?" The Prophet ﷺ said: { Then your mother. } The man asked again: "Then who?" The Prophet ﷺ said: { Then your father. }**[1]

(Please visit **www.islam-guide.com/women** for more information on women in Islam.)

The Family in Islam

The family, which is the basic unit of civilization, is now disintegrating. Islam's family system brings the rights of the husband, wife, children, and relatives into a fine equilibrium. It nourishes unselfish behavior, generosity, and love in the framework of a well-organized family system. The peace and security offered by a stable family unit is greatly valued, and it is seen as essential for the spiritual growth of its members. A harmonious social order is created by the existence of extended families and by treasuring children.

How Do Muslims Treat the Elderly?

In the Islamic world, one rarely finds "old people's homes." The strain of caring for one's parents in this most difficult time of their lives is considered an honor and a blessing and an opportunity for great spiritual growth. In Islam, it is not enough that we only pray for our parents, but we should act with limitless compassion, remembering that when we were helpless children, they preferred us to themselves. Mothers are particularly honored. When Muslim parents reach old age, they are treated mercifully, with kindness and selflessness.

---

(1) Narrated in *Saheeh Muslim*, #2548, and *Saheeh Al-Bukhari*, #5971.

In Islam, serving one's parents is a duty second to prayer, and it is their right to expect it. It is considered despicable to express any irritation when, through no fault of their own, the old become difficult.

God has said:

> ❰ **Your Lord has commanded that you worship none but Him, and that you be kind to your parents. If one of them or both of them reach old age with you, do not say to them a word of disrespect, or scold them, but say a generous word to them. And act humbly to them in mercy, and say: "My Lord, have mercy on them, since they cared for me when I was small." ❱** *(Qur'an, 17:23-24)*

What Are the Five Pillars of Islam?

The Five Pillars of Islam are the framework of a Muslim's life. They are the testimony of faith, prayer, giving *zakat* (support of the needy), fasting during the month of Ramadan, and the pilgrimage to Makkah once in a lifetime for those who are able.

1) The Testimony of Faith:

The testimony of faith is saying with conviction, *"La ilaha illa Allah, Muhammadur rasoolu Allah."* This saying means **"There is no true god (deity) but God (Allah),**[1] **and Muhammad is the Messenger (Prophet) of God."** The first part, "There is no true god but God," means that none has the right to be worshipped but God alone, and that God has neither partner nor son. This testimony of faith is called the *Shahada*, a simple formula which should be said with conviction in order to convert to Islam (as explained above on pages 52-53). The testimony of faith is the most important pillar of Islam.

(1) For more details on the word *Allah*, see the next to last paragraph of page 47.

Chapter 3
General Information on Islam

2) Prayer:

Muslims perform five prayers a day. Each prayer does not take more than a few minutes to perform. Prayer in Islam is a direct link between the worshipper and God. There are no intermediaries between God and the worshipper.

In prayer, a person feels inner happiness, peace, and comfort, and that God is pleased with him or her. The Prophet Muhammad ﷺ said: { **Bilal, call (the people) to prayer, let us be comforted by it.** }[1] Bilal was one of Muhammad's ﷺ companions who was charged to call the people to prayers.

Prayers are performed at dawn, noon, mid-afternoon, sunset, and night. A Muslim may pray almost anywhere, such as in fields, offices, factories, or universities.

(Please visit **www.islam-guide.com/prayer** for more information on prayer in Islam.)[2]

3) Giving *Zakat* (Support of the Needy):

All things belong to God, and wealth is therefore held by human beings in trust. The original meaning of the word *zakat* is both 'purification' and 'growth.' Giving *zakat* means 'giving a specified percentage on certain properties to certain classes of needy people.' The percentage due on gold, silver, and cash that have reached the amount of  about 595 grams of silver and kept for one lunar year is 2.5%. Our possessions are purified by setting aside a small portion for those in need, and, like the pruning of plants, this cutting back balances and encourages new growth.

A person may also give as much as he or she pleases as voluntary alms or charity.

---

(1) Narrated in *Abu-Dawood*, #4985, and *Mosnad Ahmad*, #22578.
(2) Or refer to the book entitled *A Guide to Prayer in Islam* by M. A. K. Saqib. For a copy, please visit the web page mentioned above.

4) Fasting the Month of Ramadan:

Every year in the month of Ramadan,[1] Muslims fast from dawn until sundown, abstaining from food, drink, and sexual relations.

Although the fast is beneficial to health, it is regarded principally as a method of spiritual self-purification. By cutting oneself off from worldly comforts, even for a short time, a fasting person gains true sympathy with those who go hungry, as well as growth in his or her spiritual life.

5) The Pilgrimage to Makkah:

The annual pilgrimage (*Hajj*) to Makkah is an obligation once in a lifetime for those who are physically and financially able to perform it. About two million people go to Makkah each year from

Pilgrims praying at the *Haram* mosque in Makkah. In this mosque is the Kaaba (the black building in the picture) which Muslims turn toward when praying. The Kaaba is the place of worship which God commanded the Prophets Abraham and his son, Ishmael, to build.

(1) The month of Ramadan is the ninth month of the Islamic calendar (which is lunar, not solar).

every corner of the globe. Although Makkah is always filled with visitors, the annual *Hajj* is performed in the twelfth month of the Islamic calendar. Male pilgrims wear special simple clothes which strip away distinctions of class and culture so that all stand equal before God.

The rites of the *Hajj* include circling the Kaaba seven times and going seven times between the hillocks of Safa and Marwa, as Hagar did during her search for water. Then the pilgrims stand together in Arafa[1] and ask God for what they wish and for His forgiveness, in what is often thought of as a preview of the Day of Judgment.

The end of the *Hajj* is marked by a festival, *Eid Al-Adha*, which is celebrated with prayers. This, and *Eid al-Fitr*, a feast-day commemorating the end of Ramadan, are the two annual festivals of the Muslim calendar.

(Please visit **www.islam-guide.com/pillars** for more information on the Five Pillars of Islam.)

Islam in the United States

It is difficult to generalize about American Muslims. They are converts, immigrants, factory workers, and doctors. This varied community is unified by a common faith, underpinned by a nationwide network of a large number of mosques.

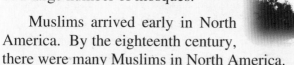

Muslims arrived early in North America. By the eighteenth century, there were many Muslims in North America.

Great numbers of Americans have entered the fold of Islam. They are from different classes: the rich, the poor, the educated, and the illiterate. Today, there are about five and a half million Muslims in the United States.[2]

---

(1) An area about 15 miles from Makkah.
(2) *The World Almanac and Book of Facts 1996*, Famighetti, p. 644.

For More Information on Islam

If you would like more information on Islam, please visit:

www.islam-guide.com/more

If you have any questions or comments, or for this book in other languages, please visit the web site of this book at:

www.islam-guide.com

For additional copies of this book, please visit:

www.islam-guide.com/copies

Also, you may contact one of the following organizations:

1) The United States:

Islamic Foundation of America
PO Box: 3415, Merrifield, VA 22116, USA
Tel.: (703) 914-4982 - Fax: (703) 914-4984
E-mail: info@ifa.ws

Islamic Assembly of North America
3588 Plymouth Road, Suite # 270, Ann Arbor, MI 48105, USA
Tel.: (734) 528-0006 - Fax: (734) 528-0066
E-mail: IANA@IANAnet.org

Alharamain Islamic Foundation
1257 Siskiyou Blvd., no. 212, Ashland, OR 97520, USA
Tel.: (541) 482-1116 - Fax: (541) 482-1117
E-mail: haramain@alharamain.org

World Assembly of Muslim Youth
PO Box: 8096, Falls Church, VA 22041-8096, USA
Tel.: (703) 820-6656 - Fax: (703) 783-8409
E-mail: support@wamyusa.org

Islamic Information Institute of Dar-us-Salam
5301 Edgewood Rd., College Park, MD 20740-4623, USA
Tel.: (301) 982-9463 - Fax: (301) 982-9849
E-mail: iiid@islamworld.net

Note: Please visit **www.islam-guide.com/centers** for addresses of Islamic centers near you.

2) Canada:

Islamic Information and Da'wah Center International
1168 Bloor Street West, Toronto, Ontario M6H 1N1, Canada
Tel.: (416) 536-8433 - Fax: (416) 536-0417
E-mail: comments@islaminfo.com

3) The United Kingdom:
Al-Muntada Al-Islami Centre
7 Bridges Place, Parsons Green, London SW6 4HW, UK
Tel.: 44 (0207) 736 9060 - Fax: 44 (0207) 736 4255
E-mail: muntada@almuntada-alislami.org

Jam'iat Ihyaa' Minhaaj Al-Sunnah
PO Box: 24, Ipswich, Suffolk IP3 8ED, UK
Tel. and Fax: 44 (01473) 251578
E-mail: mail@jimas.org

4) Saudi Arabia:
Alharamain Islamic Foundation
PO Box: 69606, Riyadh 11557, Saudi Arabia
Tel.: (966-1) 465-2210 - Fax: (966-1) 462-3306
E-mail: haramain@alharamain.org

World Assembly of Muslim Youth
PO Box: 10845, Riyadh 11443, Saudi Arabia
Tel.: (966-1) 205-0000 - Fax: (966-1) 205-0011
E-mail: info@wamy.org

For Suggestions and Comments on This Book

If you have any suggestions or comments on this book, please send them to the author I. A. Ibrahim at:
E-mail: ib@i-g.org • Tel.: (966-1) 454-1065 • Fax: (966-1) 453-6842 • PO Box: 21679, Riyadh 11485, Saudi Arabia

Also, if you would like more information about Islam or if you would like additional copies of this book you may contact the author.

For Further Reading on Islam

The True Religion, by Bilal Philips.
This is the Truth, published by Alharamain Islamic Foundation.
The Qur'an and Modern Science, by Dr. Maurice Bucaille, edited by Dr. A. A. B. Philips.
Towards Understanding Islam, by Abul A'la al-Mawdudi.
Life After Death (pamphlet), by World Assembly of Muslim Youth.
The Muslim's Belief, by Muhammad al-Uthaimin, translated by Dr. Maneh al-Johani.
Interpretation of the Meanings of The Noble Qur'an in the English Language, by Dr. Muhammad Al-Hilali and Dr. Muhammad Khan.

For a copy of any of these books or pamphlets, please visit **www.islam-guide.com/books** or contact one of the organizations listed on pages 69-70.

References

Ahrens, C. Donald. 1988. *Meteorology Today*. 3rd ed. St. Paul: West Publishing Company.

Anderson, Ralph K.; and others. 1978. *The Use of Satellite Pictures in Weather Analysis and Forecasting*. Geneva: Secretarial of the World Meteorological Organization.

Anthes, Richard A.; John J. Cahir; Alistair B. Fraser; and Hans A. Panofsky. 1981. *The Atmosphere*. 3rd ed. Columbus: Charles E. Merrill Publishing Company.

Barker, Kenneth; and others. 1985. *The NIV Study Bible, New International Version*. Grand Rapids, Michigan: Zondervan Publishing House.

Bodin, Svante. 1978. *Weather and Climate*. Poole, Dorest: Blandford Press Ltd.

Cailleux, Andre'. 1968. *Anatomy of the Earth*. London: World University Library.

Couper, Heather; and Nigel Henbest. 1995. *The Space Atlas*. London: Dorling Kindersley Limited.

Davis, Richard A., Jr. 1972. *Principles of Oceanography*. Don Mills, Ontario: Addison-Wesley Publishing Company.

Douglas, J. D.; and Merrill C. Tenney. 1989. *NIV Compact Dictionary of the Bible*. Grand Rapids, Michigan: Zondervan Publishing House.

Elder, Danny; and John Pernetta. 1991. *Oceans*. London: Mitchell Beazley Publishers.

Famighetti, Robert. 1996. *The World Almanac and Book of Facts 1996*. Mahwah, New Jersey: World Almanac Books.

Gross, M. Grant. 1993. *Oceanography, a View of Earth*. 6th ed. Englewood Cliffs: Prentice-Hall, Inc.

Hickman, Cleveland P.; and others. 1979. *Integrated Principles of Zoology*. 6th ed. St. Louis: The C. V. Mosby Company.

Al-Hilali, Muhammad T.; and Muhammad M. Khan. 1994. *Interpretation of the Meanings of The Noble Qur'an in the English Language*. 4th revised ed. Riyadh: Maktaba Dar-us-Salam.

The Holy Bible, Containing the Old and New Testaments (Revised Standard Version). 1971. New York: William Collins Sons & Co., Ltd.

Ibn Hesham, Abdul-Malek. *Al-Serah Al-Nabaweyyah*. Beirut: Dar El-Marefah.

The Islamic Affairs Department, The Embassy of Saudi Arabia, Washington, DC. 1989. *Understanding Islam and the Muslims*. Washington, DC: The Islamic Affairs Department, The Embassy of Saudi Arabia.

Kuenen, H. 1960. *Marine Geology*. New York: John Wiley & Sons, Inc.

Leeson, C. R.; and T. S. Leeson. 1981. *Histology*. 4th ed. Philadelphia: W. B. Saunders Company.

Ludlam, F. H. 1980. *Clouds and Storms*. London: The Pennsylvania State University Press.

Makky, Ahmad A.; and others. 1993. *Ee'jaz al-Qur'an al-Kareem fee Wasf Anwa' al-Riyah, al-Sohob, al-Matar*. Makkah: Commission on Scientific Signs of the Qur'an and Sunnah.

Miller, Albert; and Jack C. Thompson. 1975. *Elements of Meteorology*. 2nd ed. Columbus: Charles E. Merrill Publishing Company.

Moore, Keith L.; E. Marshall Johnson; T. V. N. Persaud; Gerald C. Goeringer; Abdul-Majeed A. Zindani; and Mustafa A. Ahmed. 1992. *Human Development as Described in the Qur'an and Sunnah*. Makkah: Commission on Scientific Signs of the Qur'an and Sunnah.

Moore, Keith L.; A. A. Zindani; and others. 1987. *Al-E'jaz al-Elmy fee al-Naseyah (The scientific Miracles in the Front of the Head)*. Makkah: Commission on Scientific Signs of the Qur'an and Sunnah.

Moore, Keith L. 1983. *The Developing Human, Clinically Oriented Embryology, With Islamic Additions*. 3rd ed. Jeddah: Dar Al-Qiblah.

Moore, Keith L.; and T. V. N. Persaud. 1993. *The Developing Human, Clinically Oriented Embryology*. 5th ed. Philadelphia: W. B. Saunders Company.

El-Naggar, Z. R. 1991. *The Geological Concept of Mountains in the Qur'an*. 1st ed. Herndon: International Institute of Islamic Thought.

Neufeldt, V. 1994. *Webster's New World Dictionary*. Third College Edition. New York: Prentice Hall.

The New Encyclopaedia Britannica. 1981. 15th ed. Chicago: Encyclopaedia Britannica, Inc.

Noback, Charles R.; N. L. Strominger; and R. J. Demarest. 1991. *The Human Nervous System, Introduction and Review*. 4th ed. Philadelphia: Lea & Febiger.

Ostrogorsky, George. 1969. *History of the Byzantine State*. Translated from the German by Joan Hussey. Revised ed. New Brunswick: Rutgers University Press.

Press, Frank; and Raymond Siever. 1982. *Earth*. 3rd ed. San Francisco: W. H. Freeman and Company.

Ross, W. D.; and others. 1963. *The Works of Aristotle Translated into English: Meteorologica*. vol. 3. London: Oxford University Press.

Scorer, Richard; and Harry Wexler. 1963. *A Colour Guide to Clouds*. Robert Maxwell.

Seeds, Michael A. 1981. *Horizons, Exploring the Universe*. Belmont: Wadsworth Publishing Company.

Seeley, Rod R.; Trent D. Stephens; and Philip Tate. 1996. *Essentials of Anatomy & Physiology*. 2nd ed. St. Louis: Mosby-Year Book, Inc.

Sykes, Percy. 1963. *History of Persia*. 3rd ed. London: Macmillan & CO Ltd.

Tarbuck, Edward J.; and Frederick K. Lutgens. 1982. *Earth Science*. 3rd ed. Columbus: Charles E. Merrill Publishing Company.

Thurman, Harold V. 1988. *Introductory Oceanography*. 5th ed. Columbus: Merrill Publishing Company.

Weinberg, Steven. 1984. *The First Three Minutes, a Modern View of the Origin of the Universe*. 5th printing. New York: Bantam Books.

Al-Zarkashy, Badr Al-Deen. 1990. *Al-Borhan fee Oloom Al-Qur'an*. 1st ed. Beirut: Dar El-Marefah.

Zindani, A. A. *This is the Truth* (videotape). Makkah: Commission on Scientific Signs of the Qur'an and Sunnah.

The Numbering of *Hadeeths*:

The numbering of *Hadeeths*[1] in this book is based on the following:

- *Saheeh Muslim*: according to the numbering of Muhammad F. Abdul-Baqy.

- *Saheeh Al-Bukhari*: according to the numbering of *Fath Al-Bari*.

- *Al-Tirmizi*: according to the numbering of Ahmad Shaker.

- *Mosnad Ahmad*: according to the numbering of Dar Ehya' Al-Torath Al-Araby, Beirut.

- *Mowatta' Malek*: according to the numbering of *Mowatta' Malek*.

- *Abu-Dawood*: according to the numbering of Muhammad Muhyi Al-Deen Abdul-Hameed.

- *Ibn Majah*: according to the numbering of Muhammad F. Abdul-Baqy.

- *Al-Daremey*: according to the numbering of Khalid Al-Saba Al-Alamy and Fawwaz Ahmad Zamarly.

---

(1) A *hadeeth* is a reliably transmitted report by the Prophet Muhammad's ﷺ companions of what he said, did, or approved of.